TO WEEP WITH THOSE WHO WEEP

TO WEEP WITH THOSE WHO WEEP

Learn to sit with another in their pain

WESLEA PIERSON

PPM

Published by Presence Pioneers Media,
Farmville, NC.

ISBN 978-1-951611-66-8

Printed in the United States of America

CONTENTS

FOREWORD

WESLEA PIERSON HAS written a helpful little book on a topic most of us would rather avoid: how to enter the suffering of others.

Our broader culture is allergic to mourning. Our instinct is to pass on the other side of the road when confronted by those in grief. Even the funeral, the most natural place for shared sadness, has been renamed a "celebration of life." We're so uncomfortable with grief and loss that even our mourning gets rebranded as a celebration.

But drawing back from suffering does not make it go away. The darkness remains, lurking in the shadows. Bitterness towards God and others festers. Anger turns to resentment, and resentment often becomes mental torment and illness. Weslea's work encourages us to resist the gravity of our culture, to face grief head-on, to weep with those who weep, bringing the power of the cross into experiences of loss and pain.

I love the supernatural church. Those who are

pursuing things of the Spirit and believe God wants to do miracles, signs, and wonders are my people. However, sometimes our belief in the power of God can make us uncomfortable with unanswered prayers, sickness, and death.

Weslea is a missionary and a supernaturalist. This book is full of testimonies of hearing God's voice, divine providence, and miraculous healing. However, as she learned on her journey, the God who heals the sick and raises the dead also allows us to experience deep places of suffering and pain.

How could we be surprised? Or have we forgotten that Jesus himself, the most supernatural man to ever live, was also "a man of sorrows and acquainted with grief?" The apostle Paul declares his driving passion "to know [Jesus Christ], and the power of His resurrection, to share in His sufferings and become like Him in death..." Paul desires to know Jesus both in the light of supernatural power and in the darkness of suffering and death. The two were never meant to be separated—they are both avenues to know the Lord. Weslea's writing reintegrates suffering and the supernatural, reminding us of the immense honor of sharing in the fellowship of Christ's sufferings.

This book is borne out of years of perseverance in affliction of various kinds: excruciating physical pain, infertility, and death. Her experiences of others giving comfort while she was in unbearable pain, both good and bad, exposed Weslea to her own weakness as a comforter. As 2 Corinthians 1:4 says, our experiences of affliction allow us to extend God's comfort to others who are afflicted. To the extent that we share abundantly in Christ's sufferings, we share in His abundant comfort.

This book contains an impartation of grace borne out of great suffering to comfort others in their time of pain. We will all, to varying degrees, "walk through the valley of the shadow of death." We will all need grace to comfort those who mourn.

As you open these pages, may your heart be opened: to confront your own suffering courageously, to enter into the fellowship of suffering with Christ Himself, and to share His comfort with those suffering around you. May joy be the ultimate fruit as you learn "to weep with those who weep."

Jonathan Friz
Presence Pioneers Media

PREFACE

I STARTED WRITING this book in 2021 after my husband's father passed away unexpectedly. I was surprised, yet again, by the wide variety of responses we received, both good and bad. This made me realize that there truly is a gap between what the Bible instructs us to do and what we actually do when encountering those in hardship. I began to gather stories, and to ponder through many of my own as well, compiling something that might give tangible and practical help to those who feel at a loss when trying to comfort others.

A year into this process, my brother Zach unexpectedly passed away. I remember it so clearly. We had come home from a small group meeting with our church and went to bed. Around midnight, my husband's phone rang. This startled us both awake. I sat up as he answered the phone and I could tell by his facial expression that something was very wrong. He wasn't responding much, just saying "Okay. What happened? Okay."

"Let me tell her."

He hung up the phone and told me that our dear friends, the senior leaders of our church network, had called to tell me my brother Zach had died. I couldn't believe my ears. I picked up my phone and called them back immediately. I was weeping. They didn't have much information and said that they had tried calling my mother multiple times with no answer. I quickly hung up the phone and called her.

She picked up within one ring and said, "what do you know that I don't?" She had just seen the multiple missed calls. I told her what they told me and we hung up so she could call them to get as much information as possible. After that call, she began to call my Dad and each of my ten siblings to let them know what had happened. The rest of the night was a complete blur.

I had experienced grief in my life prior to that point, but this was the closest and most painful. I remember going to my living room to weep, write and pray. The next morning, we packed up and headed to New Hampshire where I experienced one of the most surreal and gut-wrenching weekends of my life.

Suffice it to say, this book was placed on hold during that time. I personally was dealing with multiple areas of grief: the grief of my husband's father passing away, my brother passing away, and our own journey of years of infertility. I don't have the words to describe what those combined sorrows felt like, but it was very heavy. Words were not helpful during that time. People who listened, shared tears and were *present* without any agenda were what mattered most. I needed a break from anyone expecting anything from me. The weight I was carrying in my heart was far too heavy already. I felt as though I would break completely if someone added just one more thing.

I leaned into Jesus, *the One Who is Comfort*, and the only One who can really turn mourning into joy. He did just that. We found out we were pregnant within a month of my brother's passing.

I personally needed time to process my pain before I came back to writing. Now here I am a couple of years later, finishing this book with two little girls squealing, laughing and crying in the background. My prayer is that it would be a blessing to those who have walked through tragedy and grief, validating their pain and the weight they have felt. As well, I pray it is an aid to any who have not known how to comfort well, don't know what to do, or how to respond when someone is weeping. I have been the person in both positions. After walking through incredibly painful situations myself, I have learned a great deal from the Comforter. I have changed as a person for the better. Grief and suffering produced in me a greater understanding of the comfort that He gives and the compassion that He feels toward us.

Though I do not wish that anyone would have

to walk through these situations, I can promise you that if you lean into Jesus, He will turn your mourning into joy. He will take every one of your tears and collect them in a bottle. *Not one is wasted.*

ACKNOWLEDGMENTS

I WOULD NOT have been able to write this book without having experienced incredibly painful situations and seasons of life. I am thankful only to this end. Thankful that God always works everything for good for those who love Him.

I am thankful for every person who came alongside me in prayer and genuine and sincere comfort during times of grief. You know who you are. *Thank you.* You taught me so much about the love of God and His nature.

I am thankful for every person who attempted to bring comfort to me, even when it brought more pain. I saw myself in you and I learned. I am thankful that you loved me and desired to help. I can see clearer now and I am thankful for you.

I am thankful for my husband, Tom. You always make a way for me to have time in our crazy life to do the things the Lord has called me to. I love you.

And to my Father in Heaven, who carried me through it all. You are my reason for all things.

INTRODUCTION

THERE'S AN INVITATION to know God in pain and heartache. An invitation to draw near to Him and experience the Comforter in a more intimate way than we ever have outside of it. Jesus never promised that we wouldn't have suffering, pain or hardship, but He *did* promise to be with us through it. He promised to comfort and give peace and bear our burdens. Without Him, we could never endure it.

I know personally that, at times, it felt unbearable even knowing He was there with me. In some of my darkest moments, the heaviness of the circumstance and the unknown weighed down on me relentlessly. But, it was precisely in those darkest nights that I learned to lean into Him. It's where I learned His nature.

This book is an invitation to truly know and experience the Comforter. You will read stories that break your heart, some that may cause anger, and others that will warm you deeply and teach you about the Holy Spirit. I hope that by the end, you will walk away knowing Him more and with a better understanding of how to express the comfort that He gives to those experiencing deep pain and anguish.

There were so many times in my life that I did not know how to comfort well; I was harsh, unfeeling, judgmental, and avoidant. All of this was very *unintentional*. I actually thought that I was comforting, I thought that I was "calling the person higher," out of depression and sadness. The reality was that I was uncomfortable with their pain. I did not understand how to relate or carry pain and sadness. I wasn't really sure if it was okay with Jesus if we felt unbearable, deep sadness. This was mostly due to where I was in my journey in knowing Him experientially. I had much internal work that needed His gentle and loving touch. It wasn't until I entered into seasons of my own grief, deep sadness and mourning that I truly began to understand. And I think this is the truth about many of us: until we experience something ourselves, it is very difficult for us to relate with others in their situation. Until we have experienced God's heart in the matter, often starting toward us, it is a challenge to understand His heart toward another and express it rightly.

My hope is that as you read the following stories, and peer into the pain and experience of others, you will understand better how to comfort with the comfort of Holy Spirit, who is *the* Comforter.

In Romans 12, the Apostle Paul is writing to the Gentile church in Rome, giving them instructions on their new life in Christ. This passage offers so much insight into what the work of the Spirit of God, the Comforter, who lives in us, produces. Before we begin, let's take a look at his admonishment to them:

Romans 12:9-17 Amplified:

> Love is to be sincere *and* active [the real thing—without guile and hypocrisy]. Hate what is evil [detest all ungodliness, do not tolerate wickedness]; hold on tightly to what is good. Be devoted to one another with [authentic] brotherly affection [as members of one family], give preference to one another in honor; never lagging behind in diligence; aglow in the Spirit, *enthusiastically* serving the Lord; *constantly* rejoicing in hope [because of our confidence in Christ], steadfast and patient in distress, devoted to prayer [continually seeking wisdom, guidance, *and* strength], contributing to the needs of God's people, pursuing [the practice of] hospitality.
>
> Bless those who persecute you [who cause you harm or hardship]; bless and do not curse [them]. Rejoice with those who rejoice [sharing others' joy], and weep with those who weep [sharing others' grief]. Live in harmony with one another; do not be haughty

> [conceited, self-important, exclusive], but associate with humble people [those with a realistic self-view]. Do not overestimate yourself. Never repay anyone evil for evil. Take thought for what is right and gracious and proper in the sight of everyone.

In Paul's letter, he is reminding them that as the church of the Living God they are to reflect Him, living a life worthy of His calling. This extends towards us as believers today. It is incredible to examine this list of exhortations in regard to bringing comfort to those who mourn. Here are just a few of the specific things that he says:

1. Love is to be **sincere** and **active**
2. Be devoted to one another with **authentic affection**—as members of the same family!
3. **Give preference** to one another
4. **Be steadfast** and **patient** in distress, devoted to **prayer**
5. Contribute to the needs of God's people, **hospitality**
6. **Weep with those who weep - sharing other's grief**
7. **Do not be haughty**, don't overestimate yourself
8. Take **thought** of what is right and *gracious*

It is incredible to me how each of these instructions can pertain so specifically to comforting one another in grief, though that is not the only context in which they are to be expressed. These instructions are to be a lifestyle for the believer, the fruit of the Spirit inside of us, our natural response. If these are not part of the overflow of our lives, then we are missing something crucial. I think sometimes we believe that we are functioning in these ways, but the experience of others would say otherwise. We think that we are "giving preference" to another, but really we are thinking of ourselves. We think we are extending "hospitality," but underneath our giving there is an expectation for a certain response from the receiver. I encourage each one reading this to take time to examine if you are being found in the truth.

Throughout this book, there will be many stories that aim to shed light on the motives of our hearts. You will note that each section will address two of Paul's instructions from Romans. My prayer is that each of us will walk away with a deepened sensitivity to the leading of Holy Spirit and the pain and heartache of those around us. This is what we are called to as children of God, *to weep with those who weep.*

PART ONE

Love Without Pretense

Embracing sincere, active love and authentic affection

My Story

IT WAS AN incredibly hot summer day, just like every other day in Haiti. I had just returned to the nation after having spent a couple of months in the United States visiting family. The following months, I would be interim director of an orphanage on the island of La Ganove in a little village called Ti Palmiste. The day I arrived, there was news of a virus spreading through the country called Chikungunya. Our small team was told that there was an epidemic. One of my dear missionary friends encouraged me to go back home until things improved. This virus was bloodborne and spread primarily through mosquitos. Its name, Chikungunya, literally meant "to be contorted in pain" and it was known informally as the "bone-breaking disease." It was an unknown virus in that there was still no cure and no medication to alleviate the pain it caused.

Typically, it would cause a person to be bed-bound

for anywhere from three to 14 days, with excruciating pain, high fever, and a possible rash. The pain could be in one or in multiple parts of the body, depending on how the virus reacted in the bloodstream.

After the initial days of infection, most people were able to stand with help and move around as the pain continued to lessen. This virus remains in your blood and could cause "relapses of pain" within the first year of infection. After the first year, for 97% of those that contracted it, there was lifelong immunity.

With all this information and a whole lot of faith, I continued on from Port-Au-Prince to the island, with the assurance that God had called me there for a reason and that He was the Healer of all disease, so I didn't need to be afraid.

Within two weeks of our arrival, the majority of the children and Haitian staff had contracted the virus. We were working non-stop in the Haiti heat to keep fevers down and to pray fervently over the children who were nearly all bed-bound in incredible pain. The three other Americans who had ventured there to serve with me all contracted the virus as well. It was terrible. Everyone was suffering and there were not enough of us to help and care for everyone in need. Then, it finally hit me.

It was about nine o'clock in the morning. I typically woke up around 4:00 a.m. and was out meeting with the staff by 6:00 a.m. Since it was nine and no one had seen me, they came looking. A staff member named Renel found me in my room on the floor on my mat. It felt like it was 120 degrees. I was confused and in incredible pain with a high fever. I couldn't speak English and was mumbling words in Portuguese and Creole. Renel grabbed my mat and dragged me outside where he proceeded to dump buckets of water on me to lower my body temperature. I couldn't move my arms or my legs, and I started crying. It was June 2014.

This began a journey far more intense than I had ever expected. From June to October 2014, I had recurring pain episodes, similar to what many others had experienced, though mine seemed to last longer than others. I continued as interim director, stubbornly pushing through all the pain in order to fulfill what I believed God had sent me out to do—and we saw Jesus do INCREDIBLE things. We saw people healed from deafness, being unable to walk, severe back and knee pain, chronic headaches and more; it was amazing!

By October, my time as interim director was completed and I was in Port-Au-Prince again awaiting direction from God. I was on a forty-day fast to seek His face and clarity when He spoke loud and clear. He told me that He wanted me to return to New York City with Street Life Ministries (SLM) for nine months of "healing." I knew that He was speaking to areas of my heart that had been deeply hurt by situations I had experienced while overseas, but I was not very pleased with this directive. I was just beginning to see God move miraculously in the villages and among the Haitians with healing and demonstration of the Spirit. People were beginning to come from other villages to find out what was happening and partake. I thought this was the fulfillment of promise! Surely He wasn't asking (telling) me to leave in the middle of all that?

But He certainly was. He told me that I would be in New York City from January to September 2015 and that I needed to "rest and receive." Initially, I disliked the news, but after several days of prayer, I reached out to my spiritual father, SLM director David Van Fleet, about a short-term return. I shared what I felt the Lord told me, and after their leadership team discussed it, they warmly welcomed me back as part of the family.

At the end of October, I left Haiti and traveled to Brazil (per the Spirit's direction), where I stayed until December, leaving just in time to be home for Christmas 2014. The entire time I was in Brazil, I did not have one pain relapse from chikungunya. Many of those who had contracted the virus with me were already fully recovered, so I thought I must be as well! By the time I arrived in the States, I had totally forgotten about it.

I visited family and church family around the holidays, then headed to SLM by mid-January 2015.

I jumped right back into service and ministry with them. I had lived and served there from September 2005 to January 2012, so it felt as though I was back in a "normal" routine. Within the first two weeks, we had done a lot of cleaning and also helped a staff member move into a new apartment. I remember very clearly, after that moving day I started to feel "under the weather." I was pretty achy, but thought it was from all the physical exercise and heavy lifting. The pain began to increase in my joints and all of a sudden I realized, chikungunya! I had totally forgotten that I had the virus.

I immediately met with David, Robin and the leadership team to discuss the situation. They had me then share it with the ministry staff. I explained that I could have relapses here and there, but it shouldn't happen too often. I shared that periodic relapse could happen, with pain lasting from one day to two weeks, though the duration was unpredictable. Everyone was very comforting and understanding in that first meeting. It was pretty shocking news and hard to understand since I appeared perfectly healthy, with no visible broken bones or physical appearance of sickness. Little did I know, this was just the beginning of my journey with severe, chronic pain.

After that meeting, I continued to try to do what I could do as part of the volunteer staff, but it became increasingly difficult. Soon, I was struggling to get out of bed. In that first month, I was in constant pain but I kept pushing through because I thought, "any day now, the pain is going to stop." After about a month, it became more and more arduous for me to get out of bed. It felt as though my bones were breaking every time I moved. Each time, the pain would worsen to the point of bringing tears, with no relief even from lying completely still. By late February/early March, Robin and another staff member suggested that I see a doctor because my condition was clearly worsening and I had never been in pain for two months straight. We all wondered if something else might be going on or if I had contracted some other sickness overseas.

My parents booked a flight to Boston and arranged a doctor's appointment for blood tests. By this point, I had to travel in a wheelchair and could not walk more than ten to twenty feet without debilitating pain. David brought me to the airport, got a wheelchair and airport assistant, and sent me off with a prayer for healing. This was my first time being in need in this way and it felt humiliating. I am not sure why, but as a twenty-eight-year-old in a wheelchair, unable to do anything without tears and pain, I felt extremely vulnerable.

Being pushed around in the airport was the first time I saw so many people stare. I tried to avoid eye contact and simply look straight ahead, but it was so difficult. I was quickly brought to my gate and left there to await boarding. Another first. I couldn't just get up to go get a coffee or walk around. I was completely dependent and they had left me alone. I felt vulnerable, and like a sideshow to those that were around me. Though many people could have been looking at me with compassion, it did not feel that way at that moment.

The hour-and-a-half wait dragged on, but eventually boarding began with wheelchair passengers, including me, going first as usual. The flight crew asked if I needed an "aisle" wheelchair to get on the plane; I had no idea what that was so I declined, thinking I could do it with some help. I mean, how difficult could it be to walk down the aisle several rows? This was my first terrible idea.

The flight attendant wheeling me to the airplane joked that he knew I was just pretending so I could get on the airplane first. He was completely saying this in pure jest, not mean in any way, but due to my emotional state, it caused the tears to flow. I felt embarrassed. Now, why would someone in extreme pain feel embarrassed? I am not sure, but it's what I felt. We arrived at the plane and he helped me up, holding my arm tightly, not knowing that it would cause incredible pain. Tears streamed down my face as I hobbled along the aisle, the flight attendants watching me with pity. I knew that man felt terrible for his comment and there was nothing I could do about it. He followed closely behind me to make sure I didn't fall, all the while encouraging me, saying it was going to be okay.

I sat down, closed my eyes, and continued to cry.

As others began to board the plane, the flight attendants kindly rearranged some things so I would have a row to myself. It was the longest, most painful forty-minute flight of my life. The combination of movement, stress, and crying—which always worsened things by tensing my entire body—pushed the pain to its worst yet. I decided to take the "aisle" wheelchair on the way out. The other passengers exited the plane and I waited. When everyone was off, I was surrounded by the flight attendants. The older gentleman that had made the comments in the beginning was right there. Before he helped transition me to the wheelchair he said, "You're going to be okay. It's going to be okay." I just nodded, still crying with no words to express, but I had been thinking, "he's a kind older man." Then he said, "No, look at me. Look me in the eyes. It's going to be okay. I see a picture of you on a journey and there is an end to the journey. You're going to make it." At that moment, I knew it was the Holy Spirit speaking through him. It hit such a deep place in me and was the first promise I held onto for my healing.

THOSE FIRST FEW months back at Street Life, I was impacted by the sincerity of their love toward me. I had been gone for a few years, yet they welcomed me back, even with debilitating sickness. I never felt unwanted or as though I was a burden to them. They patiently walked me through some emotional healing I needed from things I had experienced overseas, as well as being sincere with their love toward me in sickness.

Merriam-Webster's Dictionary defines "sincere" as: *free of dissimulation (honest), free from adulteration (pure) and marked by genuineness (true).* This is what they demonstrated toward me in action. It was not in word only, but in the way they treated me, prayed for me, counseled and even served me when I could not do it myself. There was nothing fake or contrived about their responses toward me and it was deeply felt on my part.

This type of sincere and genuine love comes from the Holy Spirit. Sometimes it is formed over years and grows through both the highs and lows of relationships. Many of us have at least a couple of relationships in our lives marked by this kind of love.

Relationships I had at Street Life were of that kind. Other times, it is a gift from Him to see someone else through His eyes—in the moment—with His love. It is supernaturally charged by the Holy Spirit in us and is born out of God's love toward us. I have experienced honest, sincere love toward people I know deeply and also toward those who I did not know at all. The root is the same. The depth of our revelation of the Father's love for us determines how sincerely we can love others. It is only in His love that we can understand the incredible, immeasurable worth that an individual has to

Him. If each person matters *that* much to God, then they must matter *that* much to me.

THEY WHEELED ME off the plane, put me in another wheelchair and as we headed to the baggage claim, I saw my Dad on his way to meet me. I burst into tears again as I saw tears coming from his eyes. He quickly took the wheelchair and said, "I'll take it from here," and off we went. I didn't see his face behind me, but I knew he was the first one to feel for me with a deep love. He didn't have to say any words; in fact he didn't. He just let his own tears flow and this moved me deeply. He helped me into the car, then the ride to my mom's house passed in a blur. Upon arrival, I faced the task of getting from the car to a bed. My journey this far had been long and painful. I desperately needed to lie down and remain still. My dad offered to carry me up the stairs, but that made me nervous for both our sakes. I smiled and said I'd take his arm instead and then we slowly and very painfully made our way inside.

My mom met us at the door and that was the second time I felt love and concern wash over me. All she said was "Oh, Lena..." (a nickname she's had for me since I was small). She took me in, brought me to my room, helped me get settled into bed, and then talked with my dad for a few moments. I lay there in a daze, wondering what was happening to me. This couldn't last too long, right? God was going to heal me soon (like.. in a day or two), right? My mind was flooded with questions as I fell into a fitful sleep.

THOSE FIRST MOMENTS of realized chronic pain were some of the hardest. I am so thankful that I have a mom and a dad who were both very sensitive to that pain. They did not try to "fix" anything. Their tears weren't for themselves or out of pity for me; they flowed from true sincerity and authentic affection. There is a difference between *feeling bad for* someone and *feeling with* someone. The latter comes from a selfless place of true compassion and is felt deeply on the receiving side. It is authentic.

My parents were extending affection toward me in my state of weakness. They took care of my physical needs and were there to hold me in the uncertainty. I honestly do not know what I would have done without them. Their care for me allowed for my walls to come down and any attempt on my part to "have it all together" was disarmed.

I will continue with more of my story as we go on,

but for now consider the implications of this type of sincere love and authentic affection while reading a few accounts from others. As you read, put yourself in their position and think about what a Romans 12 type of response might have been.

Hannah's Story

IN 2005, MY husband and I took a leap of faith, leaving our home and extended family in New Hampshire with our four kids to start anew in Maryland for a new job at a church. My husband had been hired as the worship pastor at a small but growing church. A week after our fourth child, a son, was born, we packed up our family and set off for our new adventure.

From the moment we arrived, our new church family embraced us. My husband got right to work, shifting the church from singing along to background CDs to live worship with a full band. Since we didn't know anyone else in the area, the church became our family. I dove in, getting our kids enrolled in school, finding doctors for the newborn and myself, and adjusting to a new life. Before long, I found my place in children's ministry and even took on video editing for the church.

Life was good, and the church was thriving. People were coming to faith, getting baptized—it was a privilege to be part of such an inspiring mission. Our children grew, Maryland became home, and church services expanded from one to two, then three, and finally four venues, each with its own band and energy. But with this explosive growth, we started to see a shift in the church's mission. Raising funds and launching new campaigns became greater priorities. Sunday attendance numbers began to feel like the measure of success. And with success came an emphasis on the "wow" factor: lights, big screens, even fog machines. But as is often the case, the focus on continual growth and performance took its toll. The church's growth began to slow, and the push to "top" the previous Sunday grew unsustainable.

My husband was working long hours, managing multiple services, leading bands with different worship styles, and pastoring his team of musicians, vocalists, and A/V technicians. After about six years, while the mission's initial excitement had faded, he still earned positive reviews and praise for his adaptability in meeting new challenges.

During this time, the staff and spouses were participating in a financial peace curriculum one morning per week. One morning, as my husband and I were about to leave our house for the course, the pastor called, asking him to attend a last minute meeting instead. This was not unusual, as with any growing churches issues and changes frequently arise. We changed our plans, I stayed home, and he headed into the office.

He returned an hour later with a strange look on his face. When I asked how it went, he said, "They let me go." I was stunned. My husband was an incredible worship pastor, the best I knew. I asked why, and he explained they'd talked in circles before finally settling on "We're moving in a different direction." Not only did they fire him, but they also asked us not to come back, supposedly to make the transition easier for his successor. It felt like we were suddenly excommunicated from a community we had poured ourselves into. People were confused, wondering where we'd gone, but no one knew the real story.

During one of the hardest times in our lives, we felt isolated and abandoned. A few close friends reached out, but the conversations felt awkward—they were asking "why," but we didn't have any clear answers. It felt like those who did reach out were just hoping to get the "scoop" on what had happened. We didn't want to speak negatively about the church, yet we had no explanations to offer.

Looking back, I realize people just didn't know what to say. What we truly needed were friends willing to ask, "Are you okay? Can we grab a coffee? How can we be praying for you? We love and miss you." Instead, there was silence. And that was the hardest part. I know this was mostly because people didn't know the full story so they chose silence over engagement.

Instead of reaching out to understand or help, we often received comments like, "Well, Pastor so-and-so must have had a reason," or "What did you do?" When we explained that we didn't know, people would respond, "Well, you must have done something." These words, though maybe well-intentioned, came across as accusatory. It was hard not to feel defensive when, while we were already hurting, others were making assumptions. It was an extremely painful process to walk through and we felt as though we walked it alone.

Katrina's Story

MY FATHER DIED when he was fifty-two years old. After several years of battling addiction, he died of a fentanyl overdose. He got high, went to bed, and never woke up. That was the worst day of my life.

The first thing I'd like to say is simply this: *grief demands to be felt*. We can try to push it down deep, to not feel, to distract ourselves. We can try to find comfort in numerous ways. But pain like that has a unique way of spilling over, breaking whatever walls we put up to guard our hearts. The more we resist it, the more pressure builds and then the river comes. Grieving my father made me question my mental stability, my faith, and my desire to live.

In these dark moments after my dad passed, well-meaning people who loved me said phrases like, "remember, we are still here for you and we love you" and "don't worry, he is in glory right now." These statements, though both valid and true, only added to the weight I was carrying. On the one hand, my grief felt too heavy for those around me and that I owed them acknowledgement for being alive and still with me. Already carrying tremendous weight, I felt added pressure to ease others' discomfort. On the other hand, constant reminders from others that my dad was in Heaven or in glory made my grief feel unjustified. It felt as though I needed to be happy because he was "in a better place," even though I was still here on earth where sadness is real. I thought I was in sin for being sad that he was gone or for missing him. In turn, I didn't feel comfortable sharing my true feelings with those people anymore. I didn't need a "quick fix"; I needed someone to listen and just be with me in the weight of my sorrow.

With no one to listen, I began to feel isolated, as though no one could understand what I was going through. I also avoided people who might try to quickly fix the situation (which is impossible, by the way). I didn't need someone to cheer me up. I needed someone who was okay with the weight of my questions and sadness; who would just hug me or hold my hand. These simple acts offered comfort and relief, letting me express my feelings through words and tears without bracing myself for either a clichéd response or correction.

I believe that only words or actions inspired by the Holy Spirit, rooted in genuine love, can ease the grief in someone's heart—nothing from man can do it. My husband said something that illustrates this: "All the things that you love and miss about your dad will be the only part of him you experience in eternity. You will never feel the hurt of his addiction again." This caused me to look forward to seeing my dad again in Heaven.

My husband was influenced by the Holy Spirit to say those words and I felt it deeply. When facing others' grief, it is incredibly important to be sensitive to the Holy Spirit and speak only in compassion and love.

Robert's Story

IN THE SPRING of 1961, when I was ten-years-old, I lost my best friend to spinal meningitis. The backstory of this tragic event goes like this: After moving back and forth to California from New England, having been enrolled in three different fourth grades that year (Randolph, MA, Santa Monica, CA, and Malibu, CA), I had learned how to make friends quickly. My friend Gene Hill lived nearby and we instantly became best buds. We were in the same grade and spent most of our time together, riding bikes, playing sports, shooting our BB guns, surfing, and just goofing off. He was the brother I never had.

My memories leading up to his death are a bit hazy but two things in particular stand out: The day I got the news and the response from my family. Gene had been admitted to the hospital, but because his parents were Jehovah Witnesses, they refused to allow him to receive blood transfusions. He succumbed to meningitis shortly afterwards and my parents told me of his death. At the time, my parents were having their own major issues. I'm not excusing their behavior, but they, like many from their generation and cultural background, were shaped by a "just deal with it" mindset. Due to this, my parents were never very good at expressing affection verbally, physically, or emotionally. When I needed it most, they offered very little.

At that time, I was devastated by their lack of comfort and support. Thoughts of suicide and ending my life were prevalent. My home life was terrible anyway and it seemed like an easy out of a bad situation. But really, how much does a ten-year-old know about life beyond the incredible hurt they may be experiencing?

Looking back, I think the lack of constant reminders of what had happened from family and friends allowed me to quickly process Gene's death psychologically and heal from the hurt I was experiencing—unlike what often happens today when it's easy to get "trauma stuck" and let our lives revolve around past suffering. Though I can honestly say that I did not experience any long-term debilitating effects, I do wonder what might have been different had my parents comforted me during that time.

I am thankful that his death helped me think a little more deeply about life and the possibility of life after death, for which I am forever grateful! My hope is that I will see my good friend again.

LET'S PROCESS THESE stories together. We will start with the first one.

When someone is navigating the pain of church hurt, there's a fine line between curiosity and genuine care. As was mentioned, sincere love is genuine—it doesn't seek information just to share with others. It cares deeply about the person(s) involved and what they might be walking through. Unfortunately, many have experienced deep grief from wounds inflicted within a church community. Though we can't assume the responsibility for someone else's pain, we can most certainly be a source of comfort in the process. That is one of our callings as brothers and sisters in Christ.

I think we often miss the opportunity to comfort others in their grief because we believe our primary calling is to bring correction. I personally operated this way for many years. It took a fresh encounter with God's love and the sting of deep grief to understand that my primary calling is to love God and then to love people; the two greatest commandments. Certainly love *does* bring correction but that is not the first thing it does. The love of God met each of us when we were bound by sin, and He died for us right there—not when we had things put together nor when we recognized His intent toward us. No, He died for us *while we were yet sinners.* He expressed true love that gives up its life for others, whether they receive it or not. He did not bring correction first, He demonstrated sincere love through sacrifice.

When we experientially know the love of God toward us in all our weaknesses, we will be able to love others through their moments or seasons of weakness and grief. In this story, the writer states that a simple phone call to check on them would have made all the difference. Instead of blurting out every thought and question you have, such as, "you must have done something wrong," think of the person and what they might be walking through. Even if they had done something "wrong," if they are in a moment when they don't recognize it, the love of God can bring powerful breakthrough.

The Bible is clear that we are to "weep with those

who weep." When someone is weeping, correction and counsel are not what they need, nor is it what the Bible instructs us to do for a reason. In Jesus' sermon on the mount in Matthew 5, He says, "Blessed are those who mourn (grieve or lament), for they shall be *comforted*." He doesn't say they are blessed because they will be corrected or counseled. They are blessed because they will get to experience the comfort of the Holy Spirit. This begs us to look at both mourning and comfort in a drastically different way, both as receiver and giver. We will all need the comfort of Holy Spirit *and* through people at some point and we will all be called upon to *give* comfort. We must understand what that is to look like.

The phrase *shall be comforted* in Matthew 5:4 is parakaléō. It literally means in this verse *to console, to encourage and strengthen by consolation, to comfort, exhorting and comforting and encouraging.* Vine's Expository Dictionary of the New Testament says of this Greek Word: *"The most frequent word with this meaning, lit. denotes "to call to one's side," hence, "to call to one's aid." It is used for every kind of calling to a person which is meant to produce a particular effect, hence, with various meanings, such as "comfort, exhort, desire, call for."*

Mourning is a call for aid, a call to one's side. It is a language in itself that calls for the Helper to comfort, to encourage, to strengthen. We are not alone when we mourn. We are blessed with an extra measure or awareness of His nearness—and how we need it in those times and seasons. To receive comfort, encouragement and strengthening in the midst of deep anguish is God's design and *His blessing*. Oh, that we would learn this in greater measure!

The second story paints this very picture. The writer's father had passed away in a tragic and devastating way. The responses she received sounded like counsel and correction instead of comfort. I think many of us feel the need to fill the silence with *something*. Oftentimes, we go directly to giving advice or trying to help the individual see clearer. When someone is grieving deeply and that grief raises difficult questions, it can be very tempting to want to ensure they "know the truth." Truth matters, absolutely. It also matters that God can handle all our questions and He is not the least bit afraid of them. The ability to sit in the questioning with someone without fear or needing to instantly answer is a Christ-like quality. God doesn't immediately answer our questions, so we should not attempt to do so for others either—especially because grief cannot be explained away.

Someone with sincere, genuine love and affection might have sat and listened, allowing the person to cry, get angry, and spill every question. There is a peace anchored to the love of God inside of us that keeps us grounded. It also helps to ground those around us. When peace replaces pressure, we become a safe place for processing pain.

The third story demonstrated how the lack of authentic parental affection during a profound loss resulted in a child having suicidal thoughts. Let that sink in. Our ability to comfort can usher in the very presence of God and provide a space for the grieving to breathe and encounter His love. Conversely, our inability to comfort can be detrimental, adding more weight and pain to an already heavy situation. Let us pursue wholeness in the love of God that we might bring others to wholeness as well.

It is important to know that we will likely never do this perfectly. So just take a deep breath. These instructions are to guide us in offering comfort. To help us see where we might need to change the way we approach those in mourning and grief. There are people who can become "grief stuck," and have no immediate desire to come out of it. That is not what we are addressing here. Those situations still require the patient, love of God, but there will be peace in our approach and not pressure to perform. Give yourself grace as you read on, letting the Lord's light illuminate every place so that you can become more like Him as a comforter.

PART TWO

The Gift of Tears

Weeping with those who weep, praying steadfastly, and walking with endurance

SEASONS OF GRIEF often include moments of deep sadness and tears. Tears are designed by God for a reason. In fact, the Bible says that He collects all of our tears in a bottle!

Psalm 56:8 AMP writes, *You have taken account of my wanderings; Put my tears in Your bottle. Are they not recorded in Your book?* In the New Living Translation, it starts with "You have taken account of my sorrows" and that He does. Ponder that just for a moment. He is not unaware of what we are going through nor is He calloused to the tears that we cry. He is intricately involved in every season of our lives because He so deeply loves us. I remember vividly a moment when I was sitting in my room at Street Life and I was crying out to God to heal me. I was weeping because I was so incredibly tired physically, spiritually and emotionally. In that moment, the presence of God came and when I closed my eyes I saw the Father embracing me. I leaned back against Him and felt peace. Almost as soon as I saw this picture in my mind's eye and felt the peace around me, I thought *How can*

You be touching me right now and I am not getting healed? A fresh wave of emotion and frustration washed over me. But He continued to hold me. He didn't answer my questions at that moment, but He was taking account of my sorrows.

Later, I was reminded of what Paul wrote to the church of Corinth in 2 Corinthians 4:17. He wrote that our light and momentary affliction and suffering are working for us to produce an eternal weight of glory. Affliction and suffering work for us. They are producing something in us that has eternal value. Suffering and pain are working for us to produce something that is not of this world. The Bible says in both Romans 5 and James 1 that trials are working out patience, endurance, and proven character. The Lord allows us to walk through affliction. He does not immediately deliver us from pain. He sees the bigger picture and what it is producing in us. It is far more valuable than we realize. It has eternal worth.

I know from experience that it is not always easy to envision the *eternal weight of glory*. In the middle of sorrow, it can seem as though we are the weakest and most useless. I think often this is because we are in a society that glamorizes external production, people who *do* over those who *can't do*. This is not the way of the Kingdom nor is it the attitude of God's heart toward us. He delights in weakness because it is there that His strength is perfected. He sees what it is producing *in us*, something that the world cannot take away. Not only that, but we can love Him from wherever we are and in whatever state we are in physically or emotionally.

When we are grieving, it is very difficult to do. Grieving beckons us to just be. To stop and feel. Though our love for Him often is demonstrated externally, it begins in the posture of our heart toward Him. Do not despise weakness. Reject the enemy's lies about who God is and about the validity of your tears. The Triune God is with us so presently in affliction and He does not despise it nor does He despise us.

Toward the end of my journey with chronic pain, I became infused with faith. The lies about God had been dispelled by the truth of what He says about Himself, not what my experience said about Him. I broke agreement with doubt, stopped questioning what His word says and chose to believe no matter what it looked like externally. For the first two weeks of August 2015, I chose to believe that God is good, that He delights to heal, that He is my Healer, and that it was time for me to be healed. Every single day, I woke up declaring that it was my day to be healed. The suffering I endured for over a year had produced in me a deep belief in God's ability and delight to heal. It exposed a belief that I held about my worth: that I was only as valuable as what I could produce for God. It exercised my faith, stretching me to believe regardless of my circumstances. It produced a deep trust in my heart toward God and taught me invaluable lessons about His comfort and love.

This was all before He miraculously healed me. (You can read the details of the healing in the epilogue). I was being transformed in the middle of pain and suffering. An eternal weight of glory was also being produced, one that I will only access in the age to come. Do not lose heart. He is working the same, and more, in you.

God is patient in our suffering. Let us be a shining example of His likeness in a world where many are grieving and in deep anguish of heart. It is only in this age that we will have the opportunity to do so. The truth is that tears of sadness were *not His design initially* for the world and they will be completely taken away at the end of this age.

Praise God!

In Revelation 21:1-4 AMP it says,

> Then I saw a new heaven and a new earth; for the first heaven and the first earth had passed away (vanished), and there is no longer any sea. 2 And I saw the holy city, new Jerusalem, coming down out of heaven from God, arrayed like a bride adorned for her husband; 3 and then I heard a loud voice from the throne, saying, "See! The tabernacle of God is among men, and He will live among them, and they will be His people, and God Himself will be

> with them as their God,] 4 and He will wipe away every tear from their eyes; and there will no longer be death; there will no longer be sorrow and anguish, or crying, or pain; for the former order of things has passed away.

What a beautiful and stunning picture. The Creator of the Universe, our Bridegroom, will come and wipe away every tear from our eyes and there will be no more sorrow. There will be no sadness, pain, or mourning. No more crying. It sounds like a dream! Notice that He won't scold us for our tears or tell us that we shouldn't be sad. In fact, if we think through the Psalms alone, we see King David mourning and weeping over many things and God doesn't just step in to stop him. The Bible says His grace is sufficient in our weaknesses (2 Corinthians 12:9). Grace is His unmerited favor. He is not afraid of our weakness. He does not despise our tears. He draws near to the brokenhearted and those who are crushed in spirit (Psalm 34:18). What an incredible Father we have! He has so much to teach us about how to approach someone who is heavyhearted and in tears.

God is not uncomfortable with sadness. He is not simply trying to "cheer us up" so that we are happy and laughing all of the time. He Himself experienced loss and sadness while He was here as a man. In fact, the Bible says in Isaiah 53:3 that He was a "man of sorrows, acquainted with grief." Jesus understands sorrow more than we can comprehend. He walked the most painful path there was so that we could experience His peace and comfort in the midst of our sorrows. He was abandoned by those closest to Him, betrayed, rejected, abhorred, mocked and ridiculed, and felt countless other sorrows.

He also experienced grief through loss of life. Most of us know the Scripture, "Jesus wept," but do we know why He did? Many have tried to explain the "why," going as far as saying that He was weeping for the lack of faith of those around Him. The Bible does not say that. Let's take a brief look at John 11:30-37 in the Amplified version and catch a glimpse of what was happening.

> Now Jesus had not yet entered the village, but was still at the place where Martha had met Him. So when the Jews who were with her in the house comforting her, saw how quickly Mary got up and left, they followed her, assuming that she was going to the tomb to weep there. When Mary came [to the place] where Jesus was and saw Him, she fell at His feet, saying to Him, "Lord, if You had been here, my brother would not have died." When Jesus saw her sobbing, and the Jews who had come with her also sobbing, He was deeply moved in spirit [to the point of anger at the sorrow caused by death] and was troubled, and said, "Where have you laid him?" They said, "Lord, come and see." Jesus

> wept. So the Jews were saying, "See how He loved him [as a close friend]!" But some of them said, "Could not this Man, who opened the blind man's eyes, have kept this man from dying?"

Jesus was deeply moved by sorrow caused by death. It moved Him so much that He wept at the tomb. It is important to note that Jesus had told both His disciples and Martha that Lazarus would rise again. He knew that resurrection was coming, yet still He wept. As you've already read and will read again, we are often told that since our loved ones are "with the Lord" that we ought not to weep; instead, we should be content and rejoice. This is not what Jesus exemplified for us. Lazarus was going to be resurrected right then and there, and yet He still wept. He was deeply moved by the sorrow.

In 1 Corinthians 15:26, Paul writes that the *last enemy* of God to be abolished is *death*. Think about that! Death is God's enemy. If it is His enemy, then it is ours as well. In fact, this is greatly encouraging! When people die, the ache inside is *not wrong*. Nor is it a sign of weak faith or emotionalism. You might wonder about the Scripture that says, "death where is your sting, grave where is your victory." How can that be so while you are also bearing the pain of death? In one sense, when we die we will not taste the sting of death; instead we will be caught up with the

Lord. The grave will have no victory over the death of a believer because Jesus already gained the victory! What incredible hope that we have. We never need to fear death. In fact, we can look forward to the day when we will see Him face to face. Not only that, but we can have great comfort in knowing a loved one is with the Lord, where there is no more weeping, pain, or bondage to sin. These two truths, however, do not in any way diminish the pain of death or the sorrow (to the point of anger) that it brings to us who are still earthbound. Jesus demonstrated that for us in His response to Lazarus' family in their moment of deep grief and questioning.

Paul also demonstrates this same attitude in 2 Corinthians 1:3-5, 8-11. He writes,

> Blessed by the God and Father of our Lord Jesus Christ, the Father of mercies and God of all comfort, who comforts us in all our afflictions so that we will be able to to comfort those who are in any affliction with the comfort with which we ourselves are comforted by God. For just as the sufferings of Christ are ours in abundance, so also our comfort is abundant through Christ.
>
> For we do not want you to be unaware, brothers and sisters, of our affliction which occurred in Asia, that we were burdened excessively, beyond our strength, so that we despaired even of life. Indeed, we had the

> sentence of death within ourselves so that we would not trust in ourselves, but in God who raises the dead, who rescued us from so great a danger of death, and will rescue us, He on whom we have set our hope. And He will yet deliver us, if you also join in helping us through your prayers, so that thanks may be given by many persons in our behalf for the favor granted to us through the prayers of many.

Paul wrote how their afflictions led him to despair even of life, and yet in these desperate situations, he came to know God as *Comforter.* He writes that it produced such a deep trust in God, that their hope would be in Christ alone. Paul did not say that he was happy during this time. This great man of faith, writer of the majority of the New Testament, wrote that he despaired of life! He faced afflictions so challenging that he wanted to die. He went on to say that it was only because of his deep anguish that he experienced the comfort Christ gives. This enabled him to then comfort others in their affliction and suffering. It doesn't say that he was able to correct them, counsel them or cheer them up. He wrote that they experienced God's comfort and then were able to pass on what they learned to those in deep pain. Oh that we would gain this lesson from the apostle.

When I was living in chronic, bone-breaking pain with chikungunya, the Holy Spirit brought me to this passage and it was as though a light switch had turned on. Why would God call Himself our Comfort if we would never need comfort? Seems pretty straightforward, but we often avoid others' pain because, deep down, we believe that joy trumps pain and that God desires us to be happy. Unfortunately (or maybe fortunately?), there is no such promise in Scripture for the Christ-follower. He promises to give us peace that passes our understanding (Phil. 4), comfort in all of our afflictions (2 Cor. 1), and joy in His presence by His Spirit (Ps 16, Gal 5), but this is not all. We are also promised suffering (Matt 5, Jn 16, 1 Pet 4, 2 Cor 4, etc.).

We get to experience the comfort that comes from God during times of suffering. Only in this age and in this world can we experience God's comfort in the midst of sorrow because, in the age to come, all sorrow and pain will be eliminated. To truly meet someone in their struggle as Christ would, we must have a right understanding of pain and suffering.

The following stories offer a small glimpse into the pain and sorrow others might carry, calling for someone—you and me—to be comfortable sitting with them in their raw, unfiltered reality.

Margaret's Story

MY HUSBAND OF twenty-four years was getting remarried and I was in shock. I did not think that this was possible and had believed that God would bring him back to our family. The night before his wedding, a group of people gathered to pray at my house, believing with me for his return. One young man who was there began to cry out to God on my behalf. He voiced all the things I was feeling and thinking and had not yet been able to articulate. He prayed with tears in front of a group of people and I truly felt that he had entered into my sorrow. I literally felt a weight lift off of me because I knew someone else felt with me and understood what I was walking through. This was someone who truly was grieving with me.

This situation greatly contrasted another I faced during this time.

Shortly after my husband had remarried, someone came up to me and said, "Well, you know you need to forgive him, right?" I am a Christian and at the time had been walking with the Lord for some decades. Of course I knew I needed to forgive him. I did not need to be reminded of this or even encouraged to do so at that moment. This left me feeling angry. Clearly, this person was not entering into my pain nor did she really understand the situation. If she had, she would have never said such a thing.

Samantha's Story

GRIEF. MINE SHOWED up in the form of pregnancy and infant loss. Prior to that, I had never really thought much about grief. Sure, older family members had passed away and I experienced sadness, but not the raw, gut-wrenching, ugliness and pain of it. The heaviness. The feeling of trying to climb a mountain each day just to survive. Day after day, I asked myself, how do I keep going? The paralyzing feeling it brought me was relentless. Grief became my companion.

As I journeyed through, I wasn't prepared to navigate with others. In fact, many of my interactions only worsened how I felt. The constant stream of comments like, "You'll have another child," "Be grateful for the one you have," "It was God's will," "Just adopt," "It's likely for the best," or "It was destined to happen." It was these and the empty, awkward silences accompanied by "I'm sorry" that were so difficult. Though there may have been truth in some of those statements, they only worsened my sorrow and desperation. I found an anger stirring within me; an anger I had not experienced before. This anger only compounded the grief.

I hadn't realized before how uncomfortable sadness makes people, especially those not directly experiencing it themselves. Those on the outside, looking in, staring at you—that's how it felt to me, at least. I didn't have any expectations on how I wanted my friends and family to respond, but I assumed they'd 'just get it.' I figured they would instinctively know how to meet me in my sadness. Instead, I was met with discomfort, avoidance, distance and the basic "thinking of you," when I was struggling just to get out of bed and face the day.

Thankfully, I found salve to my soul in a tribe of women who were walking through (or had walked through) a similar experience. They sat with me and, even in the silence, there was comfort. They asked about my babies. They weren't afraid to remember them, or to talk about my shattered dreams and hopes for them. These women were not afraid to listen while I processed the trauma that accompanied the losses. They shed tears of sadness with me, for me and for my babies. They were gentle, compassionate, and tender. They reminded me to take care of my physical well-being, helping when I couldn't help myself. They walked beside me, held my hands and carried me at times. I collapsed in their arms because I knew it was safe. They were comfortable with the deepest parts of my grief, even though it was not their own.

They even listened as I wrestled with God. All the questions, the doubt, the anger. It wasn't met with the cliché sayings about God that we often use when we don't know what to say. I was reminded that God was also weeping with me. That He didn't "wish" death upon my babies and that He, too, was there, just as my tribe of women were physically present. He was present in my grief. I realized that's what I needed. I needed my God, my friends and my family to be present, to walk beside me, carry me, encourage me, and listen, offering grace and compassion.

In my story, the greatest comfort came from those who had walked a similar journey to mine. This was an incredible blessing and gift. Yet on the other hand, I do believe that we can offer comfort even if we haven't had a similar experience. Grief is different for everyone. It feels different. It can show itself differently, but our responses are often similar. I will never understand why I experienced pregnancy and infant loss. And I'll never be grateful for it, but I am grateful that I understand grief differently now. It has the ability to draw us closer to God or farther away. I know I always want to be a part of drawing those closer to Him, in the utter depths of grief, darkness and pain. In the midst of it, I couldn't understand how "God is always good," but as my pain has shifted I can see a bit more clearly. God was good and God is good. He never left my side and that was the very thing I needed as I entrusted my babies to Him.

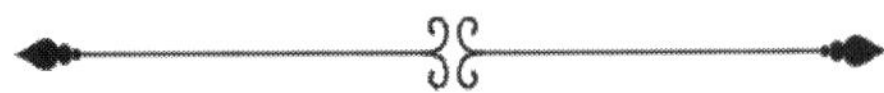

Kelly's Story

When I was first married, I remember receiving constant comments about how cute our future babies would be and questions about when we'd have one. People often said things like, "I just can't wait for your babies" or "I can't wait to be a grandma, auntie, etc."

I had this "life plan" that I assumed would naturally unfold: I would have four children, be a stay at home mom, etc. But then it took longer than expected. We were trying everything to conceive while it seemed so effortless for others. Month after month, year after year, I experienced the ebb and flow of hope and disappointment. Then, the silence came.

People stopped making the comments about babies arriving or how cute they would be. Soon, there were no comments made by anyone anymore. Silence. That was probably one of the hardest parts of facing infertility. It can be excruciatingly painful to attend baby showers or hear pregnancy announcements. And while sitting in those showers in the silent pain, no one ever came up next to me and said "I know this must be hard for you, how are you doing?"

People may believe it's a sensitive or private area to ask about, which it is. But, for me, it would have been so powerful in those moments of pain to feel seen and known by someone. It would have been so comforting to have someone bravely reach into my pain with a simple, caring question rather than constantly facing silence. There is great loneliness and repeated disappointment in infertility, intensified by the strong God-given desire for a child. To have someone who refused to be silent through the ordinary moments of life, who chose to walk with me through both the dark moments and the light ones would definitely have made a tremendous difference.

IN THESE STORIES, did you note how the writers shared that having someone comfortable with the pain was and would have been the most helpful thing in their situations? In the first one, someone entered into her pain in prayer and weeping. When she didn't yet have words for what she was experiencing, the prayer of a friend voiced every thought. In the second story, the writer found a group of women who had walked through the same painful experience as she had and those were the ones who knew best how to respond. She writes how they were able to sit with her in the pain without offering answers, but just being with her and acknowledging the loss.

In the third story, the writer expressed how she would have valued people who could share her pain and been comfortable asking how she was doing. How insightful. It sounds like what they all desired is what Jesus had given Lazarus's family and what Paul described. Someone to come alongside and feel the pain with them, to bear the burden by being present without presumption. *Someone to weep with them.*

"Tears are the silent language of grief." This quote from Voltaire hits a target. When there are no words, tears can express our deepest feelings and emotions. *If tears are a language, then the response must be in the same language*. We would never respond in English to someone speaking French. There would be no understanding, no relating, no influence. We must meet people where they are and speak a language they will understand.

And yet, even here, there is a massive difference between simply crying when someone is crying and truly entering into someone's grief and weeping with them. The difference is sincere love and considering the grieving person's needs; it is about them and not about us. Sometimes we cry because we have a relationship with the person and we are processing our own grief alongside their pain. This is not wrong in the least! It just needs to be done on our own time and not with the person grieving. The next two stories will illustrate what I am describing. Both of these situations happened while I was bedridden, dealing with chronic, excruciating pain.

My Story

ONE DAY, I was sitting in a chair in my room at my mom's house. Most days, I would stay in bed as long as I could. When I felt up for it, I would hobble across the room to sit in a chair by an electric fireplace. That was my routine for months. People would occasionally come visit me, but I quickly asked my mom to act as a shield for me. How awful, right? My mom literally needed to protect me from visitors because so many times it did more harm than good. One of those times, a dear friend came in, unannounced. I wasn't ready for this visit, and with the constant pain I was enduring, it took significant mental and emotional preparation to visit with someone.

She came in and immediately burst into tears. I had no tears. She started voicing how awful this was and began to ask why God wasn't healing me, unloading all her questions right onto me. Of course, I'm *sure* she did not realize that she was doing this. She was clearly verbally processing which I understood to a degree. I was not upset or angry, but I was absolutely tired. I felt like someone was pulling on me to comfort them even though I was the one who was sick and in constant, excruciating pain.

She stayed for probably ten minutes before my mom came and I quickly gave her the "please-save-me" look. She understood and began an attempt to usher the person out. She wanted to pray for me. My stomach turned. Most that know me, know that I *love* prayer, as did this person. So, again, understanding why she was praying, I didn't protest, but inside, I was on the verge of panic. She began to pray and cry out to God, asking why this was happening and begging Him to heal me. I felt miserable. I was already wrestling with a pile of my own unanswered questions, pressing on me like a blanket of despair and depression. I definitely did not need anyone else's added to my load. She finished praying. I was sitting there, unmoved, annoyed, frustrated, more depressed than before. She left and then I felt anger.

I was angry that she showed no sensitivity toward *me.* I was angry that it seemed like she needed an outlet for her pain and used me, with little, if any, consideration for how I was actually feeling. This is a different type of tears. Her tears weren't wrong at all, but I think they were misplaced. Those who love us deeply *will* share our pain in times of grief, sickness, and struggle, but there should be a filter to ask: Am I the one grieving here? If so, I need to process it with *someone else* or with the Lord before I visit the person who needs comfort.

Let me share a contrasting story in order to show the difference I'm talking about.

During the time that I was bed-bound at my mom's house in New Hampshire, one of my sisters came by nearly every day with my nephew. It was really nice having them there during that time as she somehow knew when to come into the room for a visit and when not to. One day, I was having a really challenging time. I was so tired of being in bed and I just wanted it all to end. During the couple months I was in NH, I tried to hold back tears when I was around people. I am not sure why, but I think maybe it was because I felt pity from so many people that I really didn't want any more. Besides, there was nothing that anyone could do anyway.

My sister and nephew were leaving for the day and I thought I was going to finally be in the house by myself. I heard a door close so I thought they had left and I began to sob. I let it all out. I could barely breathe and was sobbing and gasping with everything I had. I felt such sorrow. This went on for about sixty seconds and out of nowhere, my sister appeared and knelt by my bed. She began to sob just as loud as I was; it makes me tear up just remembering it. At that moment, I knew somehow she felt my pain. We sobbed together for probably thirty seconds and then I felt peace wash over me. No words were exchanged during that time. She said, "I love you, Weslea," got up and walked out of the room. I was left with tremendous peace.

This was the first time I experienced what I believe Romans is talking about, when it calls us to "weep with those who weep." There was something so selfless and real about her getting on her knees beside me. I knew she was not weeping for herself or for her own grief, I could literally feel it. She was weeping with me. She was not afraid of my pain. She was not trying to fix my pain. She was feeling my pain with me.

Comfortable enough to just sit with me in it until it subsided. The tears were not on her terms, they were on mine. I knew she would weep while I wept and stop when I stopped. She was truly there for me.

I LEARNED SO much from these two experiences—lessons that I will never forget. Now, when I come across someone walking through a deeply painful experience, I work to process my own pain before I reach out to them. I am deeply aware of the need to simply be with the person without adding any of my own heaviness to theirs. I want to be able to listen with clarity and compassion, not bringing any mixture from my own emotions or processing. This takes time, thought and effort. I am not saying that we will always perfectly comfort others, because I certainly believe we can and will fall short. But by being more intentional, we will hurt people much less and be more of a comfort and place of solace than not. People will come to you if you become a safe place for processing.

In the process of writing this book, I had shared the above excerpt online to give a taste of the book. A couple months later, I was contacted by someone who had read it and, shortly afterward, found herself in a similar situation. The person had been given a coupon to a department store she rarely visited and decided to stop in there. As she was shopping, she passed by a changing room as a woman emerged, clearly looking for the people she had come with. The woman asked her to help zip up the outfit, which she quickly did and told her the outfit looked great. The woman then shared that she had just lost her child and would be wearing the outfit to the funeral. She broke down weeping. She instantly wrapped the woman into her arms and began to weep with her. They were like that for a minute or so and then the woman said "Wow, I really needed that. Thank you." The person told her that God must have sent her there because she doesn't usually shop there. This warmed the woman's heart and they parted ways.

The person called me to tell me this story. She shared that she had been raised in a home where emotion was rarely shown, nor was comfort offered when there was sadness. It was a "pull yourself together" type of home. Because of this, she normally was very uncomfortable with sadness, often trying to "fix" the situation, which didn't usually end well. She was confronted by the excerpt I posted and something "clicked." So much so that when she encountered this woman in a very real and present situation of grief, her automatic response was to simply be with her and to weep with her.

That is my hope for each person who reads these stories. Let us learn the language of tears.

Paul's Story

IT WAS SHORTLY before 11 p.m. on April 27, 2022, that I received a call I'd hoped would never come. My son, my beloved son Zachary, had died.

This is an account of a life event I would rather

not have to bring back and rehash because along with the memories come some of the raw emotions and mental anguish that accompany them. The incredible grief and sadness that only parents who have lost children know. And the questions. Why, Zach? How, as his father, could I have altered his course in life? How much had my choices affected Zach's? On and on the questions come. But face them I must.

Obviously, it was a tough time for our whole family. No one is evwer prepared for news like this even if the history of the deceased would say different. I can clearly remember the outpouring of love and support I received from both relatives and friends and even some who were not too friendly towards me. It was both encouraging and loving. At the time, I had a former brother-in-law who was still extremely upset with me about my divorce from his sister. However, when I walked into the church the night of the memorial service, he at once came over, put his arms around me and expressed a genuine, heartfelt sorrow for me. His words were kind and compassionate and the moment seemed to take away all the animosity he had towards me.

And how could I not include the reconciliation that took place between me and my oldest son. He and I had not spoken to each other for ten years. We had a major falling out years earlier over some business issues which led to the breakdown of our relationship. When Zachary passed away, a family gathering took place at my oldest son's home. I was extended an invitation to join and when I arrived he was sitting on his deck with friends and family around him. My son was heartbroken and sobbing when I walked up the back steps to the deck. As I approached him he stood up, and for the first time in over a decade, we embraced, both of us expressing through tears our remorse for each others' loss. Sadly, it took the death of someone we both loved deeply to bring the birthplace of reconciliation to an otherwise dead and broken relationship.

Grief is a funny thing. It can hit you at any time, anywhere, under any circumstance.

Some months later we were visiting friends in the Chicago area and on a Sunday in July, went to their church, Willow Creek. Near the end of the service, as we were walking out into the large foyer, the thought of losing Zach hit me like a ton of bricks. I broke down and just began weeping like I had never done before. My wife wrapped her arms around me and tried to console me as I wept on her shoulder. My friends appeared, asked what was wrong and immediately began to pray for me. It took a few minutes, but in retrospect, I understand that a grief hitherto not expressed was released from me. I was so thankful to have my wife and friends there to help me through an incredibly painful time not so much with their words but just with their presence. Once again, I thank the Lord for the way He uses people as vessels of encouragement and love in some of our darkest hours. And above all, for the sure and certain hope I have because of Jesus in seeing my son again.

REMEMBER, WE ARE only gifted tears in this lifetime; in the age to come there will be no more tears and no more sorrow. It might sound strange to call them a gift, but that is the truth. They allow us to express and release deep, inner sorrow. Harvard Health wrote an article explaining the science behind tears. In one section it states,

> Scientists divide the liquid product of crying into three distinct categories: reflex tears, continuous tears, and emotional tears. The first two categories perform the important function of removing debris such as smoke and dust from our eyes, and lubricating our eyes to help protect them from infection. Their content is 98% water.
>
> It's the third category, emotional tears (which flush stress hormones and other toxins out of our system), that potentially offers the most health benefits. Researchers have established that crying releases oxytocin and endog-

> enous opioids, also known as endorphins. These feel-good chemicals help ease both physical and emotional pain.[1]

God designed tears to help our physical bodies deal with the stress of grief and to combat heaviness by releasing oxytocin, "the love hormone." It is incredibly healthy to cry. In many ways, our culture has suppressed tears, and the Church has not escaped this reality. We are told not to be overly emotional, not to waste our tears, to hold things together, etc. This is not God's intention toward us! He actually created us with the gift of tears so that our bodies could feel a sense of relief when processing through painful situations. Never be ashamed to cry!

Like we read in the last story, it is also vitally important that we don't hinder others from crying in moments of deep heartache. When we enter into their pain with them and when we understand the gift of tears, we will willingly and naturally weep with those who weep and something supernatural takes place. Often, a greater measure of comfort and release comes when someone weeps with you concerning a matter. It destroys the lie that we are alone in our pain. It leaves no room for the enemy to steal from and further isolate us from community. When we weep with those who are weeping, we are inviting

---

1 https://www.health.harvard.edu/blog/is-crying-good-for-you-2021030122020

them into the deepest sense of community and profound brotherly love. It will cause them to draw near to community instead of running away.

PART THREE

Open Hands, Open Heart

Giving preference to others and extending true hospitality

Fernanda's Story

MY HUSBAND'S FATHER passed away unexpectedly. It caught us completely off guard. He had gotten sick and quickly took a turn for the worse. Many stood in faith, praying for his healing and recovery, but it did not come. One day he was here with us and the next he was gone, with no medical explanation for this turn of events. There were weeks of endless tears, wondering how and why this could have happened. In that time of questioning, several people tried to explain it to us as a family—and that was excruciating. Death cannot be explained away and even a valid reason does not take away the feelings of immense pain and loss. Statements like "I don't know nor do I understand, but I am so sorry you have to walk through this," were some of the most helpful and comforting things to hear. It validated our questions without giving any sort of theological reason for his passing or why God didn't heal him; it was a loving and supportive statement that held no judgement and did not attempt to "fix" anything.

When we arrived home from the memorial service, we stepped inside to find our kitchen counters overflowing with cards, flowers and food. While we were away, our church family had filled our fridge, bought us groceries, prepared meals, and showed their love through cards and flowers. We both wept as we saw it and read everyone's heartfelt messages. This was such an act of love and lifted a huge burden of meal preparation off us. The last thing we wanted to do was think about meals or grocery shopping. It was a tremendous blessing.

Melissa's Story

I COULDN'T BREATHE when I heard the diagnosis. There was nothing more that could be done medically. It was impossible. I was too young. I had too much left to do. God loved me and promised me a hope and a future. What kind of future could I have blind? My daughter had never seen me cry as hard as I did while she drove me home from the eye doctor on a cold and gray Thanksgiving Eve. I've been grieving in one way or another since that day, for the past two years. It's not the loss of a loved one that has caused the grief. It's the loss of sight. And all the subsequent losses that come as a result of that.

Driving. Being a rock star at work. Managing my household. Reading mail. One by one, my freedoms and abilities were stripped away. Things I had often taken for granted: Independence. Daily five-mile walks. Reading price tags. Sunshine without sunglasses. Clipping my own nails. The assignment of labels: Significantly disabled, requiring accommodations, legally blind.

Often I would remember the testimony of a friend's healing and my hope would be renewed, but every time I got my balance, another layer was stripped away.

Loss of social interaction. Loss of understanding the visual nuances of movie storylines. Loss of seeing my daughter's smile across the kitchen table. Loss of reading books to my grandkids. Loss of noticing facial expressions and body language. Loss of color.

It feels like the hits keep coming and coming. And even as they do, God is ever present, holding me so tenderly. Giving and blessing and comfort even as the losses pile up. God's hand is clearly evident in the midst of my trials. My son came home from his own dream and calling of African missions to support his widowed mother. A man of honor, strength and Godly character who I am proud and grateful to call my son.

Sweet and loving grandchildren living in the same house as me, not overseas. And a beautiful, faithful daughter-in-law who is committed to raising lovers of the Lord, who gave up her mission dreams as well to return to her husband's childhood home. My daughter who serves and honors me daily and lives a life laid out on the altar. Who set aside her own desires to live at home and help me, acknowledging my new limitations without letting me wallow in them. A church that offers me ways to serve actively without taxing my eyesight, giving me a vital sense of ongoing purpose and connection. Friends who show up faithfully to drive me to church, to our Friday breakfasts, on errands, or just to come and spend time with me.

These are tremendous blessings, people who have met me in the pain and loss, provided both practical and spiritual support. They have encouraged me in my faith and have brought much comfort amidst the loss.

WHEN WE SHOW up for each other, even in practical ways like making meals, there is a demonstration of love that goes far beyond what words could ever offer. This is a picture of showing hospitality by contributing to the needs of the saints. If you've ever lost a loved one, endured chronic pain or dealt with grief, you would likely agree that people delivering food or helping out in other ways, without any expectation or strings attached, is a tremendous blessing.

If you have not experienced that level of grief, it might be helpful for you to understand that most people feel so completely overwhelmed that food is the last thing on their minds. It is common to forget to eat, let alone find the energy to plan meals or grocery shop. If you have a family with children, this can be even more challenging! Receiving meals over a period of time alleviates just one of the many practical things that still need to be done. Many say they're too overwhelmed to even identify what help they need, and the greatest relief comes when people simply show up to do laundry or clean, or send groceries and restaurant gift cards without asking what's needed.

These are invaluable gifts that do not go unnoticed and express love that comes straight from the Father's heart. Not only that, it is also fulfilling the second greatest commandment: to love your neighbor as yourself. Do you remember the story of the Good Samaritan? Let's read the story that Jesus uses to explain loving our neighbor.

Luke 10:30-37 AMP:

> Jesus replied, "A man was going down from Jerusalem to Jericho, and he encountered robbers, who stripped him of his clothes [and belongings], beat him, and went their way

> [unconcerned], leaving him half dead. Now by coincidence a priest was going down that road, and when he saw him, he passed by on the other side. Likewise a Levite also came down to the place and saw him, and passed by on the other side [of the road]. But a Samaritan (foreigner), who was traveling, came upon him; and when he saw him, he was deeply moved with compassion [for him], and went to him and bandaged up his wounds, pouring oil and wine on them [to sooth and disinfect the injuries]; and he put him on his own pack-animal, and brought him to an inn and took care of him. On the next day he took out two denarii (two days' wages) and gave them to the innkeeper, and said, 'Take care of him; and whatever more you spend, I will repay you when I return.' Which of these three do you think proved himself a neighbor to the man who encountered the robbers?" He answered, "The one who showed compassion and mercy to him." Then Jesus said to him, "Go and constantly do the same."

This is an incredible story. In it, the priest and the Levite (who were ordained specifically to minister to God) are the ones who passed by on the other side. Sounds like avoiding another's pain and suffering has been a common practice for quite some time. We don't know the specific reason why they passed by on the other side, but we do know that there was a lack of love and compassion, which would have compelled them to stop.

The Samaritan, who was considered unclean by God's people, was moved with compassion. He did not pass by. He saw him and was deeply moved. So much so that he spent a lot of time and money to ensure that his every need was met.

Jesus' response was to instruct us to constantly do the same! Be ready to give freely and joyfully to those around you in pain and suffering. Being filled with the Father's love equips us to respond immediately with compassion in action, especially in an unexpected situation. It takes time and effort to love someone well in the middle of pain and loss. Be encouraged! In this, you will be fulfilling the second greatest commandment.

This story shows a beautiful picture of generosity. The Oxford dictionary defines hospitality as "the friendly and generous reception of guests, visitors and strangers." That sounds just like what the Good Samaritan did. He acted as a dear friend to a complete stranger who was in a very desperate situation. He provided all that was necessary in order for that stranger to receive the healing that he needed. In this situation, it was food, lodging and anything he may have needed. We are commanded by our Lord to do the same.

Hospitality requires acknowledgement. It requires us to stop, listen, see, and act with compassion. More often than not, people suffer in silence due to fear that others will hurt them more. When you are walking through painful situations, it may feel like you have an open wound. We all know that when we have physical open wounds, we protect them at all costs. If I have a cut on my hand, I can feel it often because I use my hand often. I will wrap that wound in gauze and do whatever I can to protect it from further injury. This is often how grief manifests as well—like we are walking around with an open wound and are overly cautious of it getting "bumped," which we know will cause much more pain.

My husband recently had a rib pop out of place. I have never gone through that myself and don't know what it feels like, but I've heard it is very painful. He was sitting on the couch talking to a friend when he coughed and it popped out of place. He had the wind knocked out of him and fell to the ground. I was sitting there, unaware of what had occurred, and began laughing, saying that he's such an old man that coughing landed him on the floor. He couldn't talk or breathe. I quickly realized that something was very wrong. We found out that by coughing, he had irritated an injury from a week earlier, resulting in his rib popping out.

For the first week or so, I was very sensitive to this. I knew that he couldn't do much. He couldn't lift our girls or do what he typically does around the house. As the weeks went on, I somewhat forgot that he was still recovering because I didn't see it as much. He looked completely normal on the outside most of the time. There were times when I would give him a hug and he would wince and then I would remember and step back quickly, apologizing for causing more pain. He needed more time to fully heal, and I needed to work on remembering that!

Though this is a true story, it could be an analogy for the wound of grief. It is quite common that after someone passes away, within the first one to two weeks, many people reach out, offering support and compassion. But after those initial weeks, most people forget and move on with their lives. Those who are grieving often feel that they walk out into the world where everyone continues their normal routines, yet their world has been completely turned upside down, and no one knows. Some might check in occasionally, but life gets busy and people forget because it did not impact them as deeply as it did you. A careless comment (like the hugs I gave my husband) can cause us to wince in pain because we are still healing. That person, most likely unintentionally, has hurt us because he is not experiencing our pain.

It takes selflessness and humility to consider what another is walking through. More often than not, when we do consider the situation, we will be compelled to do something to bless or encourage the individual. It can be as simple as dropping off a meal or sending a text or as extensive as doing laundry and cleaning the house. The story of the Good Samaritan gave us a great picture. We are providing space for the individual to heal with the least amount of responsibilities as possible, if possible.

Kathryn's Story

WHEN I WAS twenty-four years old, my husband and I were trying for our second baby. Our first child was only a year old and we had gotten pregnant with her very quickly, without any issues. Due to this, we thought having a second one would be just as simple. We got pregnant and we were so excited to give our first child a sibling. We felt like it was great timing and we were so ready for that next step. We reached out and told our family and our friends and began to celebrate this new life that was growing in my womb. We were already envisioning what life would be like with two babies growing up together and all that we could do as a family.

When I was about seven weeks pregnant we went in for our first ultrasound, excited to see our little nugget! As we watched, the ultrasound technician seemed to be searching around my stomach for a while. My husband and I looked at each other and we could just sense that something was off. We could see the sac on the screen so we knew that I was pregnant (I also had tested positive on multiple pregnancy tests prior to this), but we weren't seeing the heartbeat. We knew it was still early, so we weren't sure if that was a problem or not. The doctor came back in and told us that they weren't seeing a heartbeat, but that it was still very early. She told us not to worry about it and asked us to come back in for another ultrasound in a couple of weeks. This made us somewhat nervous, but we asked our family to pray. We were praying that somehow it was a mistake that they didn't see it and that when we returned all would be normal.

When we returned for another ultrasound two weeks later, we felt very tense in the room again. We could feel something was off. The doctor came in and told us she was sorry and that they didn't see any heartbeat. She explained that there would have been growth by now and there hadn't been. I was miscarrying the baby. My husband and I looked at each other in shock, not quite sure if we should believe this news. We had only heard stories of miscarriage. Could this really be happening to our child? The doctor began to explain possible next steps —that I could either have a D&C or allow it to happen naturally. We decided to pray for a miracle and let it happen naturally if we didn't receive that miracle.

I was still feeling all the pregnancy symptoms (nausea, exhaustion, etc.) at about twelve weeks in. We were at my in-laws and that's when it began. We rushed home to our house which was a few hours away, by the time we got there I felt as though I was in full-blown labor. It was absolutely horrible. I delivered the placenta and miscarried and was left with a hole in my heart. Leading up to this, someone had said to me, "you know, you're going to be fine. It will just be a heavy period." This was the furthest thing from the truth. After I had spent four hours laboring, I began to feel so angry and hurt by what people had said to me, comparing the loss of my baby to a heavy period.

The miscarriage felt isolating. I remember lying in bed that night and I just sobbed. I could not stop crying. I felt as though I had no one to talk to; I had never experienced this amount of pain before. That pain and grief lasted for months. It affected my relationship with my husband and our communication as we were grieving in different ways. I felt as though I had no one to talk with because of some of the initial responses I had received. Looking back, I think what would have been most helpful and consoling would simply be acknowledgement. Acknowledgment of the pregnancy, our baby, the miscarriage and the pain we were walking through. I think that could have come through texts or phone calls; simple things that would have pulled us gently into relationship, leaving an open door for conversation if we needed or wanted it.

Jacob's Story

SUSAN WAS OUR local mom.

When we moved into her region to pioneer a new ministry, she greeted us with gifts, tears, prayers, and encouraging prophetic words. She was the type of person who would arrive unannounced with six bags of groceries or spend an entire day cleaning our house to bless my wife who was overwhelmed with our growing family.

Paul, her husband, was a mentor and father figure who I loved. We had served together in various ministry capacities for years, and I deeply respected his leadership. I anticipated we would be kingdom partners for life.

Then, things changed.

Our team was handling a case of spiritual discipline in our local ministry. Susan, familiar with the person involved, sought to prescribe exactly how we would respond, despite not being on the leadership team. We recognized the gravity of the situation, but our decisions were not severe enough for Susan. I even consulted other pastors, questioning if I was mistaken, but they confirmed we were handling it correctly and that Susan was overstepping.

She requested a meeting. With Paul looking on, she cursed us, forever breaking fellowship. It felt like an excommunication, except it didn't make sense, because we were not under her authority. Her actions shook our fledgling ministry which was still in its early stages. As a result, we had to shut it down just months later. Our team, who had moved to pioneer this new work, was deeply shaken and discouraged by what had transpired.

The effects of this betrayal lingered for years. Most people didn't know what had happened and I chose not to share details to protect Paul and Susan. While the fact that most people could not understand the pain was difficult, there was an added depth of fellowship among the few who went through it together. One of my ministry partners who was also very close to Paul and Susan would quote this Scripture to me, "though father and mother forsake me, the Lord will take care of me." I also knew that Susan had done what she did from a place of deep brokenness.

A few years later, I had a severe illness and received an unexpected outpouring of love from the community. I remember thinking "this illness is less painful than many other forms of suffering, because at least everyone understands what you are going through."

About a year later, I was on sabbatical in another part of the country. I saw a man who looked like Paul at a restaurant, and my body immediately went into fight or flight mode. And then, it hit me. I was thousands of miles away. Paul was not around. I felt rest enter my soul. God was giving me space to heal.

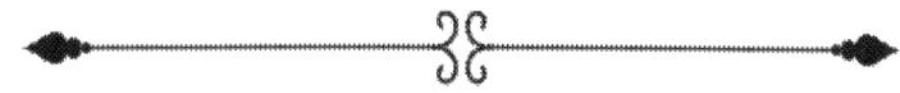

Mark's Story

YEARS AGO, I owned a construction business. I had one partner, a very close friend. Our families had even purchased land and built our homes on it together. I trusted him deeply. After some time, we added another partner to the business for cash flow purposes. Though he was a relative of my initial partner, I did not trust him. After he joined the company, my responsibilities began to change as the two were giving me more and more tasks that they did not want to do.

Over the years, the company grew substantially. However, numerous relational issues were accumulating and left unresolved. One day, a significant issue arose on a job site. I had a prior commitment we all knew about. I was unable to get to the job site. I fulfilled the commitment while my partners went to the site. The problem was so severe that they had to work late into the night to resolve it. To be clear, this was a normal aspect of our business.

For years we operated this way, with many instances where I addressed issues without them as well.

The next day, the two of them called me into a meeting where they berated me for not helping with the issue. I reminded them why— a reason that we had all known and understood. This did not matter to them. I left the meeting feeling a profound sense of betrayal and hurt from their words about me.

We met again and I shared what I was thinking. I spoke primarily to my original partner and close friend; I still did not trust the other man. I shared very openly, with tears. I reminded my original partner of the countless times I had covered for him, and never said anything about it in our years of doing business together. I told them that if they wanted my resignation that I would give it that day. They did not accept it and we worked together a couple more years, despite continuing relational issues. Then, my family and I felt the Lord calling us to move to another state.

As we prepared to move and leave the business, my partners agreed to buy out my portion of the business. Our CPA estimated the fair price of my interest in the business, yet the two offered me ten percent of that amount.

For me, this led to yet another feeling of betrayal. My approach to business partnerships is full transparency. I went above and beyond numerous times to ensure they received what was due them. I wanted

God's blessing, so I never even considered withholding money from them. This was not mutual and I later learned that they had withheld from me on multiple occasions.

At that time, I sought counsel from my pastor. He stated that it didn't matter whether they paid me fully or not because I knew what God was calling me to do—move to another state. Although I didn't fully understand his counsel, I still received it. I accepted their offer and sought peace to remain in relationship with my original partner, despite the deep betrayal in our business separation. I knew it was what God asked me to do.

I quickly realized that doing the right thing does not reduce the sorrow. I entered into a deep depression. I believe a professional diagnosis at the time would have concluded that I was clinically depressed.

A calling to the marketplace can closely resemble a calling to pastoral care. I am responsible for the people that work for me and I care deeply for people. In both business and ministry, there is opportunity for betrayal—I would even say that it is inevitable in both callings.

There is a deep measure of grief that comes from betrayal. Few in the church understand how to deal with betrayal in the business realm, although it is not that much different than in a church community. This makes it difficult to find sound counsel from church leaders. I often wondered where I could find godly business leaders who could provide mentorship.

Fortunately, my family has some strong believers who offered me counsel and encouragement.

I would like to say that God turned everything around and honored my obedience. I now have several thriving businesses, with Him as my partner in each one. He uses our brokenness to cause us to trust Him in new ways and follow Him in new paths. For that, I am truly grateful.

THESE STORIES DEMONSTRATE how grief has a unique ability to either bring us into isolation or into deeper relationship. I believe that God intends for it to be the latter. As we have seen in these many different stories, it is very easy to become isolated. If we are hurting and someone says something to further that pain, we may want to build walls so that pain doesn't happen again. Though this is completely understandable, it is not the better way. Isolation can cause us to get stuck. We get stuck in the pain, with lies continually invading our minds and hearts, and it seems nearly impossible to get out.

We need God and we need people. I am not saying that it is someone else's responsibility to keep us from isolating. I am saying that it is extremely helpful when others recognize this tendency and offer their presence, even if quiet, when someone is in pain.

In the first story, the writer desired deeper connection, but was wounded by the things that some had said. She ended up feeling more isolated due to the lack of care and interaction from those around her. How powerful would it have been if her miscarriage had been acknowledged for what it was: loss of precious life. How powerful if a few people showed care through a meal or conversation or doing something to provide space for healing, like we saw in the story with the Good Samaritan. Her healing may have come much quicker if she had received that kind of response.

In the two stories about betrayal, it is evident that they both felt more pain even though they did the right thing. The more pain came because each of them kept the details to themselves and only shared them with a handful of trusted people they were in close relationship with.

In the ministry story, this brought the individual into closer relationship with those friends who walked with them through the situation. It brought a measure of comfort to know that at least someone knew what they were going through, even though there was still increased pain that most did not know what really had happened.

In the business story, the betrayal happened over a period of ten years doing business together. The writer didn't realize how much it had affected him until he found himself in a deep depression after his move. He desperately needed mature believers to mentor him in the business realm and he found none. Thankfully he had some family members to encourage him, but this type of experience can so easily bring an individual into isolation and make it that much more difficult to trust.

The enemy often comes when we are in very real and horrible situations. He takes the opportunity to "kick us while we are down," so to speak. He does this through lies that we believe because of what is happening around us. If we are isolated and not in communication with others, it is that much easier to believe those lies and not even realize that we are! It is so important as comforters to realize the power of connection and relationship, even if we don't know the intimate details of a situation. To reiterate, experientially knowing the love of God will help us to overflow in this area as a response.

When I was bedridden with chikungunya, it was very easy for me to listen to the voice of self-pity. The cycle for me began as "God is going to heal me, I have no doubts!" Then, "God must not like me, He doesn't hear me, people avoid me, I'm going to be like this forever, I don't want to see or visit with anyone because they are just going to hurt me more." Then back to "God is going to heal me, I have no doubts!" That cycle spanned seven months and as much as I would like to blame my lowest moments on other people, I cannot. I chose to listen to that lying voice for many months. I isolated myself at times because I simply could not handle someone else hurting me.

I remember on one of these self-pity days, I was sitting outside in the sun, home alone with depressing thoughts. It was a beautiful day and I couldn't move. I was in extreme pain and thinking about how no one my age (twenty-eight at the time) should be in this situation. As I was ruminating, my mom came home. I didn't hear her, but she came looking for me. She came outside and asked how I was doing. I must have given some depressing response because she immediately said "That's it! We are going to the park and we are going for a walk. It's a beautiful day." I was horrified. No, Mom, I do not want to "go for a walk," which consists of you pushing me in a wheelchair, at some park.

She didn't back down. She helped me up, put me and my wheelchair in the car, and off we went. We went to a nearby park and she began pushing me on the walking path. I was absolutely miserable. I was seeing everyone walking, running, playing ultimate frisbee. All of a sudden, someone comes running up to us. I didn't recognize him, but it happened to be someone from my church. A bunch of guys were there playing ultimate frisbee. "Great," I thought. I didn't want to see anyone and now this kid who I barely know is approaching me to make small talk. (This "kid" became my husband just a short three years later...oh how the Lord works.)

I let him talk mostly with my mom until someone I knew better ran up to us. A dear friend. I started talking to him and spilling how awful I was and how much life sucked at the moment. It is so interesting how getting outside in the sun and seeing a dear friend started to change my attitude. Moms are always right! Especially my mom. My mom and I have a close enough relationship that she could make this "executive decision" and know that it was right for what I needed. I needed sun, fresh air, a change of scenery, and friends (who the Lord provided as a surprise). On that day, I was in the mood to isolate, but isolation would have only exacerbated all the lies taking up space in my mind and heart. I needed relationship, friendship, and conversation. And many of us need just that.

This might sound silly, but it was on that walk that the kid I barely knew got my phone number from my mom so that he could help out in some way. A couple days later, I received a text from him that made me laugh out loud....and the rest is history. We became the best of friends and then we got married. Oh how the Lord works in grief and heartache! Oh how His intentions toward us are much better than we could ever imagine. In the middle of suffering, it can be very hard to accept the truth that He is absolutely incredibly good, but on the other side, it all becomes much clearer how He would not waste one tear.

God is a God of Redemption. Do you remember

the story above about the loss of one son that ended up bringing a restored relationship to the other son? Or the story of the loss of a father-in-law and brother that ended up bringing years of infertility to an end and the first miracle child? God does redeem every part of our stories as we continue to put our lives into His hands. If you don't quit, you will win. It will look different for each one of us, but it is so important to realize that if the situation does not look good, it is because He is not done yet.

PART FOUR

Wisdom in the Quiet

Choosing humility and thoughtfulness and resisting arrogance

RECALL WHAT ROMANS said that we are to "take thought" to what is right and gracious, to not be haughty and arrogant, but to pursue humility. Comforting someone else in deep pain or distress has nothing to do with us and all to do with the other. It requires time, consideration, and thought. We can't go about it haphazardly or with yourself in mind, it requires us to be humble, thinking of the other, and it requires us to know God.

Paul had just exhorted the Roman church to be transformed by the renewing of their minds, to avoid thinking highly of themselves, as we are all part of One Family and One Body, deeply interconnected. We must have a "Christ-centered" and "Family-centered" approach in our comfort where it has less to do with me than it does the person in front of me. This is true, selfless love and it will be felt by those around us.

Here's a story of mine to help illustrate what **Paul is talking about.**

IN 2021, MY husband lost his father unexpectedly. I rushed out to Arizona to meet with the family as his health was declining quickly. As I was being dropped off at the airport, at 4:30 in the morning, I slammed my left, middle finger in the truck door. It was shut completely in there for a solid five seconds. I got it out, it was instantly black and blue, bleeding and bent, but I had to get on that plane. My husband needed me there and I urgently had to go. The guy from our church dropping me off prayed for me and then I was off, a seven-hour journey with a damaged, throbbing finger. I found out a week later that it had broken in three places.

My broken finger affected everything for months. It hurt all the time; I couldn't sleep well, cook, wash dishes, wash my hair, or drive without it swelling incredibly and causing pain. But what did I expect? I had broken it. The fingers surrounding it hurt the most. There was nerve damage and swelling and none of them could move well. My mind was constantly preoccupied with it, paying attention to keep it elevated and away from being unintentionally hit. I had neck and shoulder pain from sleeping weirdly so that it wouldn't get hit in the night. Everything revolved around this broken finger for months.

I began to think of the passage of Scripture that says when one hurts, we all hurt as we are one Body, all connected. I thought of how appropriate that was for the season I was in. Not only is it absolutely true in the natural with our physical bodies, but it was happening right before my eyes. My husband, my in-laws, and I were all hurting and it was felt by those around us, by dear friends, family and church family. Those closest to the immediate family felt the pain and were affected by it the most. There was real pain all around. Real grieving by many. Being part of the Family of God means deep connection. For this reason, when someone dear to us is hurting, we feel pain as well.

Unfortunately, many church communities today just have "services" with few opportunities for true fellowship. We cannot deeply know a brother or sister in the Lord if we only see them for an hour or two on Sunday. I think this is a major reason why we don't weep when others are weeping: we don't care deeply for one another because we don't really know each other. We only know each other on a surface level. This will just not suffice.

Relationship is key to not only feeling with someone in a moment of pain, but also being with them. Relationship draws us in through invested time, emotion, and thought. It is where real love is developed. Having a deep relationship with the person and deep relationship with the Father will make the greatest difference. Comfort given in love and with sincerity and thought for the person in pain will be felt deeply by the recipient.

Many times, I experienced both love from someone I had deep relationship with as well as pain caused by lack of relationship/no thought given to my situation. The following stories from others will help show the distinction.

Deborah's Story

"ARE YOU GETTING over it yet?"

I was asked this question a few months after my mom passed away. I know this question was well-intended, but it was very hurtful. Death of a loved one is never something you get over. It got me thinking though about whether the person asking had any idea of what I was going through.

The loss of someone you care about leaves a place in your heart that can never be filled the way it once was. That pain always stays with you. The pain of never being able to talk to them again, hug them again, hear the family stories you grew up hearing, never tasting the food they made, nor being able to make the food they made because you never got the recipe from them. That person in your life was irreplaceable and the memories are forever a reminder of the good times that once were and that you wish you could have back. That loss is something you have to live with every day and does not go away.

Thoughtfulness is key when asking someone how they are doing. Even the way a question is worded should be done with care.

Ted's Story

WHEN MY DAD passed away I was hours and thousands of miles away from my friends and support system (aside from my wife, mom, and sisters). It was unexpected and devastating. Many people offered condolences with phone calls, texts, and messages, but, over and over, words continued to fall short of easing the pain. I think most people know that anything they say cannot truly reach the depth of pain someone experiences in a death of someone close.

Grief will ultimately run its course, no matter what people say. In my experience, the things people said to me just left me feeling awkward and did not lessen the pain, albeit with good intent and compassion. I understood, and regardless of the awkwardness, I was appreciative of people's words.

One thing stood out to me the most in those days immediately following the passing of my dad. Some close friends heard about what happened, and, without a second thought, drove six hours from San Diego to Tucson to be with me. Not to offer condolences or to try to coddle me in my pain, not to try to fix the situation or to sweep in like a hero, but to just be with me as my friends. That offered me a sense of normality that I so desperately needed at that time. I needed something that felt good and familiar and didn't remind me of what happened (because everything reminded me of it), all while validating my feelings and proving their love and support.

They didn't try to pretend it didn't happen by not talking about it. Everyone knew what happened and that I was in pain, but by not talking about it and just being with me, they gave me room to breathe and to talk about it on my terms if I wanted to. That meant so much to me during that time — the action that proved their condolence. They didn't need to say anything or try to make me feel better — even though that's our natural inclination when people we love are going through grief. We think, "let me fix it!" But they just came selflessly and were normal, which was exactly what I needed.

They let me go through my grief, but were normal!

Elizabeth's Story

MY SIBLING PASSED away very unexpectedly. It caught us all by surprise and the grief that came was so unpredictable. I had been invited to a friend's wedding that was scheduled only a month after he died. I wrestled with the decision to go. I was not sure if I would be in a celebrating mood nor was I sure I would want to be in a large room with many people I know that knew he had just passed. I weighed the decision for days and decided to go at the last minute.

My husband and I arrived and I did pretty well

at first. One of my close friends asked how I was doing and I appreciated it even though I immediately welled up with tears. Her eyes also filled with tears and I was able to tell her that I couldn't talk about it and that we needed to change the subject fast. Because she was such a close friend to both me and my family, this did not offend her at all. She immediately understood and within seconds she had me laughing about something totally unrelated. Phew, that was a close call, I thought.

As the reception began, I found myself feeling more and more weighted down with sadness and really wanted to leave. I got my husband and told him I needed to quickly get to the car. He said he would be right there so I left. As I was walking to the car, an acquaintance called out to me. I stopped for half a second, but I was on the verge of tears so I was praying that they wouldn't try to talk with me for a long time.

They said they heard about my brother passing and that they were sorry. They then shared that they thought he was such a funny guy and had always made them laugh. They began to laugh as they shared this and I was not prepared for that. I just nodded and said I had to go, as I rushed to the car crying. I felt upset because they didn't really know my brother or my family.

As I was processing this entire scene later that week, I realized a few things. I realized that I probably didn't make the best decision in going to this event. I wanted to be okay, but I probably rushed myself and that was something personal. I also realized the difference between the two encounters I had. I was completely fine with the first interaction because it was someone that I knew very well and who also knew my sibling very well. I knew that I could be honest and she would respect that without offense. Sometimes it is just as simple as depth of relationship that will make the difference in knowing when and how to approach the interaction.

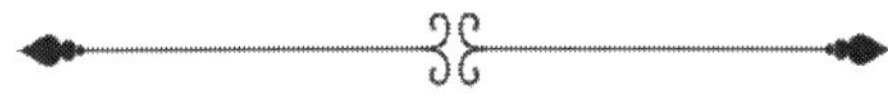

Jennifer's Story

AS A PERSON with numerous chronic health issues, there is a fine line you have to walk. If you are not active at all, you end up with more health issues. Your body deteriorates. But at the same time being active is hard. You have to push through pain, balancing issues and extreme exhaustion. If you push too much, you suffer even worse because your body just goes crazy. Then you are out of commission for weeks and have to start at the beginning with physical therapy and you never make progress. It's a very, very discouraging situation and extremely unhealthy.

One day, a woman from a church nearby came to see me. She told me that I needed to not let the symptoms control how I live. She said I needed to believe and speak healing over my body, which I had been doing for a very long time. She said I really needed to step out in faith and do things that I wasn't physically able to do. Many people have said similar things to me. Sometimes I would feel as if I had to prove to people that I was actively wanting to be healed and to live life. I would push myself to do something and then I would be bedridden for weeks. This happened on numerous occasions.

Patricia's Story

AS A SINGLE woman I was wishing I could have someone to share life with. To eat dinner with. To talk to. To pray with. I mentioned this desire to a friend who responded with "Jesus is your husband and He's the only husband you will ever need." That comment was very hurtful.

David's Story

WHEN I WAS 23 years old, I was dating a girl whose dad was the senior pastor of a church. The youth group of the church wasn't doing too well, so her dad stepped in to help out. He was headed to pick up supplies when he was tragically killed in a car accident. What I remember most is that many people were saying "life is but a vapor." I probably heard it about fifty or sixty times during the short period following his death. I understood that these people were also grieving, trying to make sense of what had just suddenly happened, but the phrase was not helpful. I think we need to be okay with not understanding why something has happened. I think it's very important that we approach people in grief in the same way. This is authentic and truthful because we don't actually know the reason why many tragic situations happen.

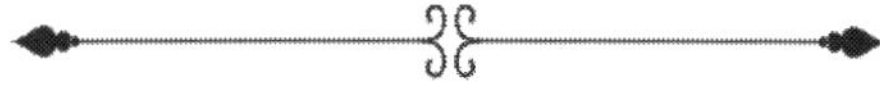

WHEN WE SAY things without thinking, in most cases, we run the risk of hurting someone deeply or saying something foolish. The Bible talks so much about this. In Proverbs alone there are over 100 verses that talk about the tongue! Here are just a few that are helpful to meditate on:

> 10:8 The wise of heart will receive commands, but a babbling fool will be ruined.
>
> 10:19 When there are many words, transgression is unavoidable, but he who restrains his lips is wise.

12:18 There is one who speaks rashly like the thrusts of a sword, but the tongue of the wise brings healing.

15:4 A soothing tongue is a tree of life, but perversion in it crushes the spirit.

15:23 A man has joy in an apt answer, and how delightful is a timely word!

15:28 The heart of the righteous ponders how to answer, but the mouth of the wicked pours out evil things.

16:23-24 The heart of the wise instructs his mouth and adds persuasiveness to his lips. Pleasant words are a honeycomb, sweet to the soul and healing to the bones.

17:27-28 He who restrains his words has knowledge, and he who has a cool spirit is a man of understanding. Even a fool, when he keeps silent, is considered wise; when he closes his lips, he is considered prudent.

18:13 He who gives an answer before he hears, it is folly and shame to him.

18:21 Death and life are in the power of the tongue, and those who love it will eat its fruit.

I remember when I was eighteen years old, I read Proverbs 17:27-28 for what seemed like the first time. I decided to refrain from speaking for a few days. It didn't work as well as I wanted because I was serving at a ministry at the time and they were wondering why I wasn't talking. I quoted the Scripture and said that even if I was a fool and kept silent I would be considered wise. They chuckled at me at the time, but I was so serious! The longer I walk with the Lord, the more I realize that less is more. When I speak too much, there is always error. This so applicable for walking with those who grieve. Please never forget: less is more!

The story we read described a young man who lost his father and the presence of his friends from California was a great blessing. The writer mentions how it was a blessing to be able to have space to talk about the pain on his own terms and when he was ready. This is so important! If we are talking too much, there will never be space for the one in grief to be comfortable to share. It is not common to want to force your way into a conversation about your pain. There must be space for it to happen. And that space is only reached when there are people who listen well and listen long.

Not only that, but it is biblical to take thought before we speak. If we are uncertain, it does no harm to pause and think and pray before taking a step. I remember when my brother passed away, someone had seen me in a public space and they had wanted to acknowledge his passing, but she waited, being unsure how or what to say. Later that day, she privately messaged me, sharing her dilemma about wanting me to know she was thinking of me. This was SO meaningful to me and is such a great example. If you want to acknowledge someone's pain (which it is clear that most of us grieving want the pain acknowledged) but are uncertain about timing or what to say, it is safe to reach out privately and share that openly!

Be mindful not to overgeneralize, as each person is different in what comforts them—that is why it is so important to know people. But I do think it is safe to say that most people would be blessed by a private message similar to what the person that wrote to me said:

> *Hey there, I just wanted to let you know that when I saw you the other day I really wanted to acknowledge your pain and ask how you were doing, but I was uncertain about how that would make you feel in a public place. So I am writing to you to let you know I am thinking about you and I am here if you ever want to talk. I can't imagine the pain you must be feeling.*

Her message acknowledged my pain in a private space that she knew would be safe. She was being thoughtful. She was considering me and my feelings and putting them first. She was slow to speak. It made a tremendous difference.

LIKE WE HAVE read, it can be common to jump to giving counsel, correction or quoting Scripture (often out of context) when someone is in deep pain and voicing questions, doubts, or anything they might be processing. For example, the story about the woman voicing her desire for a husband. For some reason, the first and immediate response was to shut down her desire by claiming that Jesus was a good enough husband. Well, duh. But if that were to be taken literally, then no one should get married. If "He is the only husband you'll ever need" was a true statement, then why has any Christian woman ever been married? And what about men? In what sense is God our husband? Is it only for females? We know biblically that is not the case. He is a Husband to His Church, His Bride. He can certainly comfort any individual who is going through divorce or loss/lack of marital relationship, but, biblically, marriage is His design and it is good.

So, why did this person respond so quickly in that way? We don't have them here to ask, but I surmise it is because we often don't fully know God's goodness ourselves, so we struggle to share it with others. When someone is expressing pain or any longing that comes from pain, we want to have an answer immediately to why it is not being satisfied. It is so important to remember, less is more. A more comforting response might have been: "That sounds like a beautiful desire, a God-given one. I will be praying with you for that." No counsel. No correction. No Scripture out of context. Just entering into someone's longing that came from a place of pain and supporting and encouraging them.

When we enter into someone else's pain, we lay

aside what we think is best and our opinions to simply be with the person, feel with them, and love them in a sincere way. When we put ourselves in their position, we can let our hearts ache with theirs, acknowledge their situation, listen carefully and sincerely, and carefully consider our response, if a response is needed.

My Story

I HAD BEEN bedridden at my mom's house for about a month. The blood test results confirmed that it was chikungunya and it was coursing through my blood. I went to several different types of doctors and kept receiving the same report: "We are so sorry. There is nothing to treat this. This is a newer sickness and unknown to us. You might need to prepare yourself to be in a wheelchair and bedridden the remainder of your life." Though I had seen God heal countless times in my years of missionary work, I began to question whether He really wanted to heal me or not. My faith was being greatly challenged.

On Resurrection Sunday, I decided to go to church. I had to go in a wheelchair and required a lot of help to get around. A friend picked me up and off we went. I was a little nervous about being around so many people who I knew would want to talk or pray with me. It might seem interesting that I was nervous about that, but it was mostly because I, unfortunately, hadn't had the greatest experiences with people up until that point.

I asked my friend to wheel me off to the side—I really didn't want too much attention on me. As we went forward to get around to the side, a couple stopped us. I had met this couple before, but did not know them well at all. They had gone to the morning service as visitors so they were on their way out as I was on my way in, but we didn't make it past them. They stopped us to say hi and, instantly, I had a very bad feeling about what was about to happen.

They began to ask what had happened to me and I shared very briefly how I contracted the sickness and what doctors were saying. I barely finished before they decided they wanted to pray over me and declare God's healing. They began to pray very emphatically and the woman grabbed my legs and declared healing. I was now crying because of pain and great frustration. They both began to cry as well and cry out for God to heal me. Then, the woman took my hands and told me to try to stand up. At this point, I told her that I couldn't. I was in so much pain and I was so upset with what was happening. She told me that I needed more faith to be healed and if I just believed more that I would be able to walk and, with that, they left.

I was so angry! I remember thinking, "I don't need more faith, YOU do!" This left me feeling exhausted, discouraged, upset, and many other emotions. I wanted to crawl into a hole and be left alone, but it was too late, I had decided to come to a church service on one of the busiest Sundays of the year.

I was not angry that they prayed for me. It was how everything took place that was bothersome to me. First of all, I did not know the couple well. We did not have the type of relationship that would give them that kind of access and boldness to speak to me that way. The entire interaction left me feeling as though they had been hoping for another "notch" on their "healing belt" to tell people they prayed for someone in a wheelchair. When I didn't get up and walk, they blamed it on me and a lack of faith on my part. Plus, they didn't know enough about the sickness to know that they shouldn't have been grabbing my legs while praying. This caused incredible pain. I also had given no permission for hands to be laid on me. I love the laying on of hands for praying and healing, but with someone you do not know well, you should always ask if they are okay with it! I would have easily said no in this case, but I wasn't given the option.

A very similar situation happened again, but with a totally different outcome. Hopefully the contrast will help in understanding why certain things might be appropriate in certain contexts and not appropriate in others.

I was in Canada, where my brother, who served at the Quebec House of Prayer, was caring for me while my mom was away on a trip. I was there for about a week and mostly lying in bed or on a mat in the prayer room.

Toward the end of my time in Canada, my mom came to pick me up during an all-day prayer burn. I had been in a lot of pain all day so I slept through many of the prayer sets on a mat in the prayer room. The following is a journal entry I wrote during this time:

> "May 2, 2015, 9:25 p.m.
>
> Today is the all-day prayer burn at QHOP. I went into a ton of pain and slept through a few of the sets on my mat. When I woke up at 6:00 p.m., Mom took me in my wheelchair to make me dinner and this Canadian couple began to talk with me and ask why I am in a wheelchair. They have been to Haiti many times. I could tell from the beginning that they are very genuine, loving believers. They asked to pray for me and it felt like such a good right thing. They began to pray and I did feel a tingling sensation throughout my entire body. There was still pain, but that tingling happened three or four times and I knew the Holy Spirit was so near. They began to prophesy over me..."

At this point in the journal entry, I went on to document the prophecy that they had given me.

I remember distinctly that as they were praying, I

felt the presence of God so richly and His love washing over me. At the end of their prayer, they asked if I wanted to try to stand up. Because of the tingling that I had felt, I did want to try! They gently held my arms as I tried to stand. I couldn't do it because of the pain, but when I sat back down I did not feel discouraged at all. They just smiled at me and told me that they sincerely believed that this would just be a season of life for me and that God was going to heal me. They encouraged me in my faith, both that I was strong in faith and to keep on believing. I left this interaction so edified.

WHAT A DIFFERENCE thoughtfulness and humility make! In both situations, I did not know the people well. In one situation, they asked what had happened to me and let me fully explain, asked if I wanted prayer, and asked if I wanted to try standing. When I wasn't instantly healed, they encouraged me and were not bothered in the least. I knew that if I said no to any of their questions, they would have gladly respected and understood. This couple was so sincere and so loving that it made a lasting impression! I will never forget this interaction and remain grateful for the encouragement I received from it. I learned from their example that day.

The first interaction also made a lasting impression, but not a positive one. There was no consideration for me, a real person sitting in front of them. It was as if I was some spiritual experiment; that if they didn't pray for me, they wouldn't have done their duty that day. They simply did not pause to think about what I was telling them. Don't hear me wrong, I'm not upset with this couple or harboring any sort of resentment. I simply learned an invaluable lesson from them also.

In my time with chikungunya, I experienced a variety of interactions, both healthy and unhealthy. Times when people forced their way in to pray with me, anoint me with oil, or cry for me. Part of the time I just didn't have the energy to set a boundary because of my physical condition. The other part of the time, I truly felt for people. I saw myself in these horrible interactions. I was so convicted of having done the same or similar things to other people in the middle of pain and I was honestly horrified. So I let them "do their thing" and I guarded my heart from becoming bitter or accusatory. I realized that I needed so much grace and forgiveness for the ways I had most likely hurt people, so I was giving them that grace and immediate forgiveness from my heart. I truly understood.

This is honestly how this book began to formulate in my heart. I realized how much I was learning by walking through these interactions. I realized how much I didn't know. I realized that I had never really understood how to comfort someone well. The fact is, I am still learning. I am still learning to love and comfort with the comfort of the Holy Spirit. This is a journey that each of us need to walk.

The instructions that Paul gave to the New Testament churches were to be handed down for all time. They are for me. They are for you. And how we desperately need them. There is an invitation to grow in the love of God for each other. To understand the great need for us to enter each other's joys and pains, highs and lows. To walk with each other in a steady and consistent way, guarding from offense and bitterness that are all too easily agreed with when in grief.

Floyd McClung says that humility is the root of all godly virtue and pride is the root of all sin. When we admit that we do not know it all and that we don't have all the answers, we are taking an honest assessment of ourselves and choosing to humble ourselves. This will have great effect. Thoughtfulness is a fruit of humility. We can only have room to think of others when we are thinking of ourselves less. Philippians 2 expresses this attitude that was "in Christ Jesus" and that we should all have. This is such a familiar passage that bears repeating.

> Do nothing from selfishness or empty conceit, but with humility consider one another as more important than yourselves; do not merely look out for your own personal interests, but also for the interests of others. Have this attitude in yourselves which was also in Christ Jesus…

The passage goes on to describe how Jesus, the

High and Lofty One, humbled Himself even to the point of death on a cross. Paul is exhorting the churches to look at the perfect example in Christ and to mirror Him. That, because of humility, we would consider others more important than ourselves and we would look out for the interests of others. This exhortation, when applied, can greatly impact the way we comfort others in distress. This, coupled with Jesus' teaching to do to others what we would have them do to us (Luke 6:31), would transform His church in drastic ways.

For myself, before I had walked through seasons of deep grief, I never really considered how I would want someone to comfort me. This is what Jesus was encouraging us to do. To think. In order to treat someone the way I would like to be treated, I must examine my heart and a situation with that in mind. Even then, we might miss it and that is okay. I probably would have claimed I was loving people well through their grief back when I was clueless, offering advice and correction thoughtlessly. Now I know from experience how I would have wanted to be treated in grief.

I pray that, whether you have experienced heartache and anguish or not, this book has helped give a glimpse into the heart of Christ toward those who are mourning; that it aided you in your journey to learn how to comfort with the comfort of the Holy Spirit; *to weep with those who weep.*

A NOTE TO THE GRIEVING

FIRST, I PRAY that in reading this book, you found your pain validated and acknowledged. I pray that you took solace in the fact that there are many others with you on this journey of encountering the love and comfort of God in the middle of deep pain and heartache. *You are not alone.*

Second, I want to encourage you to guard your heart from offense and bitterness while you grieve. As we have read, and probably have experienced, we are clearly learning how to comfort as Jesus would and are sorely lacking. We must give grace to one another. This can be extremely challenging when you are already walking through your own pain, but it will be worth it. I experienced deep sorrow walking through chikungunya, the passing of my father-in-law and brother, and years of infertility. I have seen how easy it can be to feel justified in offense and bitterness, but it only isolates us more and causes barriers in relationships. It is not worth it and will not help in our healing journey. Here are some things that I learned in my journey and I pray they help you in yours.

- **Understand your own limits.** If you need help creating a boundary, talk with someone you trust in order to make one. When I had chikungunya, I told my mom I needed her to help keep visitors at bay. We had a secret signal so that when I needed visitors to leave, she knew and could usher them gracefully out. Sometimes we just need help from someone who will understand.
- **Lean into relationship.** With the above being said, connect with those you share deep relationships with, even if they're not the most skilled at comforting. The relationship in itself will help guard against bitterness and offense. Community is a gift from God. Let people in, even if it feels scary at times. We don't want to build unapproachable walls around ourselves. It will also be a lot easier to tell someone who you know well when you need space again.
- **Be gracious and understanding.** I know this can be a tough one especially when we are carrying so much grief already, but it is extremely important. When someone says something to you that should not

have been said or prays for you in a way that offends rather than heals, give it immediately to the Lord. Forgive the person in your heart and release them to Jesus, acknowledging that *most likely* you have done the same thing to someone else unknowingly. We are all in a place of learning and growing and we all need a lot of grace and forgiveness. People *will* hurt you unintentionally, but remember, it's unintentional.

- **Give yourself grace.** You are going through an incredibly difficult time and I want you to know that it is okay to not be okay. It is okay to be sad, to get angry, to have questions. It is okay to vent, to not have the answers, to cry and cry and cry some more. It is okay to need space and time to process, it is okay to want to process with other people. It is okay to feel extremely tired and to not "volunteer" or be involved in life's events as you normally would for a period of time. It is okay. It is also okay to get involved or be active if that helps in your journey and processing. Each person is very different and may need different things in the time of healing. The important part is to process and not avoid what has taken place in your life. However you can do that, do it fully.
- **Lean into Jesus.** This is probably the most

important thing you can do while in grief. He has given us the Holy Spirit as Comforter and He is perfect at it. There is no need to over-spiritualize the season by attempting to create reasons for whatever is happening in your life. He understands even when we do not. He sees our coming and our going, our rising and our sitting, He understands our thoughts from afar; He is near and He is good. Blessed are those who mourn, for they shall be comforted.

A NOTE TO THE COMFORTERS

I PRAY THAT this book has helped you to understand what some are walking through when in grief. I would like to highlight the key points that can be carried with you on your journey of learning to *weep with those who weep.*

DO's

- Listen well, listen long. Give time to the grieving to share what they are walking through. Don't interrupt. Give plenty of space for them to fully express their thoughts and feelings. Avoid sharing your own experience without invitation. An example could be "I have been through something similar, I'm so sorry you have to walk through this." If they then ask for you to share, the door is open.
- If needed, allow yourself time to grieve be-

fore going to comfort someone in their grief. In this way, you'll be certain you won't be adding any weight you are carrying to theirs.

- Instead of asking what they need, examine the situation (or ask someone else that knows them better but is not the griever). Clearly communicate what you'll be doing (i.e. I'm going to deliver dinner on this day, I am going to send you groceries, what day would that be most helpful, let me watch your kids so you can have time to process, I would like to clean your house OR make you meals, which would you prefer, etc.)
- Always ask before you pray for the person, lay hands on them, etc.
- Sending a private text can be helpful if you are uncertain about time and place. As we saw in many stories, acknowledgment was one of the key things that people desired in deep distress. Acknowledgment of their pain, loss, distress. This can be done in person or through text and, if you are unsure, privately is better!

DO NOT's

- Avoid giving counsel and correction unless asked for specific advice.
- Don't try to answer the questions that are made in the griever's time of processing (un-

less directly asked your thoughts and even then be cautious to not make up answers to fill a void.)

- Never place blame for "lack of faith," instead encourage their faith and remind them how loved they are.
- Be sure to avoid using Scripture out of context to make blanket statements. If you don't know what to say, just listen. Phrases that are typically helpful include: "I am so sorry you have to go through this." "My heart is breaking with you." "I don't understand either." Don't be a "know-it-all!"
- Don't show up unannounced. Most are already carrying a lot and having someone show up, especially if there is an expectation to visit, is too overwhelming. Unless you have deep enough relationship that they could tell you it's not a good time, always ask first.
- Don't assume you know what the person is going through, even if you went through something similar. Every person and every situation is different. Comforting someone in grief has nothing to do with you and everything to do with them. Avoid talking about yourself and what you would do or your experience. Humility will go low and give thought to the person in front of you.

EPILOGUE

AUGUST 12, 2015

I was praying and the Lord spoke to me and said, "Run. I am going to heal you while you run." I had been believing for healing and attempting to exercise my faith by doing things I couldn't do before. Nothing as big as running though. I was attempting to lift my water bottle to my mouth or walk to the bathroom without help. This instruction seemed very big to me. I knew that if I attempted to run and my healing didn't come, I would be in such excruciating pain for days. I asked the Lord to give me confirmation if this is what He truly was saying. I needed it.

AUGUST 14, 2015

I was in unbearable pain lying on a couch, crying. I had been believing for healing every day since the first of August and it hadn't come yet. As I was talking to the Lord, I heard Him say to me, "Rest, today is your last day in pain." I so desperately wanted to believe this. I hobbled to my bed and fell asleep, wondering what the next day might hold.

AUGUST 15, 2015

I woke up and was not healed yet. I wondered if I heard God correctly. I hopped on a FaceTime call with my parents to discuss my future steps, since God had only told me to remain at Street Life until the end of August. As we were talking, one of my sisters walked into the room and onto the call. She said, "Are you healed yet?!" to which I responded "Not yet." Everyone was believing with me for an "any day now" healing. My sister proceeded to tell me that three days prior (on August 12) she was praying for me and the Lord told her to tell me to go running and that He would heal me while I ran. I was blown away. My faith immediately surged and I told her that I heard the same thing on August 12.

I told them that I was going to put my sneakers on and go attempt to run. We hung up and I began to prepare myself. I texted the ministry leaders and staff and asked them all to pray as I was going to attempt to run.

I hobbled outside and at the end of the driveway I took a deep breath and began to "jog." I write that in parentheses because I don't think anyone watching me could discern that I was trying to run. I was still in pain so I probably looked like I was hobbling along. I reached the end of the road and turned onto the main road. I was perplexed as the pain was not increasing, which was the first miracle, but it was still present.

I began to say out loud, "Lord, You said that if I could run You would heal me. I am here, heal me!" At that moment, I felt all the pain travel from my feet up through my body and out. That is the best way I can describe it. I realized instantly that the pain had left my body and I began to cry and shout and wave my arms around. I was in complete shock and incredible joy filled my soul!

Before I had finished the call with my sister, she had said, "when God heals you, testify immediately!" I am eternally grateful that she said that because it was then the first thing in my mind. Less than a block ahead of me a man was walking and I knew that I needed to tell him what happened. I ran up to him. The back of his shirt read "Hellbound." I laughed at this! Thousands of people from many different nations had been praying for me to be healed and yet this man was going to be the first person that God wanted to hear about it. He would no longer be "hellbound."

I ran up to him, sobbing and flailing my arms. To this day I wonder what he must have thought. I tapped him on the shoulder and he looked bewildered when he turned around. He asked if everything was okay. I excitedly told him that I had been in a wheelchair with a disease that was incurable and that God had just healed me. He was clearly skeptical. I mean, we were in Queens. Crazy stuff happens in NYC all the time. I asked him if he had any pain in his body. Again he looked at me skeptically, but told me that he did. He shared that he had a 20-year-old shoulder injury that prevented him from lifting his arm up beyond a horizontal level, which he proceeded to show me.

I told him that I believed that God wanted to heal him and asked if I could pray for him. He said yes with hesitation. I placed my hand on his shoulder and said something like "be healed in Jesus name." I honestly can't remember exactly because I was very focused on the fact that I still had no pain in my body. As soon as the words left my mouth, his arm shot up into the air. Completely vertical. He was shocked and proceeded to ask me again what happened to me. I think he finally believed that I had been telling the truth.

I told him that Jesus loves him and that he should find a church somewhere to learn more about God's love for him, but that I had to keep running and telling others what had just happened to me. Off I went.

I ran a mile that day and stopped many times along the route. I will share one last encounter from that run just because it was so incredible to me.

As I was nearing Street Life, I saw a UPS truck and was compelled to jump into the open door, literally. So I did. One of the workers was sitting there and he was very startled, but also curious. I excitedly told him that God had just healed me, that I had been in a wheelchair earlier that day with a disease that was incurable. He burst into tears. He proceeded to explain that he was a backslidden Christian and that he had asked God that morning to give him a sign that He was real and here I came jumping into his truck. I laughed, told him that God loved him, jumped out of the truck and finished my run. There is a video and some pictures of me running into the driveway. The staff was ready to record my healing if it came, and it did!

God's timing is absolutely perfect. Countless people who were on that mile route that morning who needed to encounter Jesus in a real way. It always amazes me to think how my pain and suffering resulted in healing for others as well. Even more incredible to me is that much of that healing was for people I had never met before. God delights to heal and He is always working. He is good and His timing is perfect.

Made in the USA
Middletown, DE
12 September 2025